KU-671-987

RITA'S CULINARY TRICKERY

FOR ECK AND LUCY

RITA'S CULINARY TRICKERY

HOW TO GET DINNER ON THE TABLE EVEN IF YOU CAN'T COOK

RITA KONIG

EBURY PRESS
LONDON

First published in Great Britain in 2004

1 3 5 7 9 10 8 6 4 2

A CIP catalogue record for this book is available from the British Library.

Ebury Press
Random House, 20 Vauxhall Bridge Road, London SW1V 2SA

Random House Australia (Pty) Limited
20 Alfred Street, Milsons Point, Sydney, New South Wales 2061, Australia

Random House New Zealand Limited
18 Poland Road, Glenfield, Auckland 10, New Zealand

Random House (Pty) Limited
Endulini, 5a Jubilee Road, Parktown 2193, South Africa

The Random House Group Limited Reg. No. 954009

www.randomhouse.co.uk

Art direction: Caz Hildebrand
Design: Julie Martin
Editor: Jinny Johnson
Illustrations: Joy Gosney

ISBN 0 09 189919 2

Printed and bound in Singapore by Tien Wah Press

CONTENTS

Introduction	7
Chapter 1 Gathering People	10
Chapter 2 Breakfasts	50
Chapter 3 Hunter gathering	74
Chapter 4 Laying the table	90
Chapter 5 The dinner party	110
Chapter 6 Cooking for children	162
Chapter 7 Celebrations	174
Chapter 8 Eating outdoors	202
Chapter 9 The sweet end	230
Acknowledgements	255
Index	256

INTRODUCTION

This is a book about friends, food and eating – not about being a great chef. Having people to dinner is about so much more than being able to produce a great feast. You can go to someone's house and eat a delicious dinner but have an awful time. On another occasion you can have a great evening and can't even remember what you ate. What is fun is who else is there.

Culinary Trickery is about entertaining as a whole. It takes a look at the bigger picture: who you have to dinner, how you create an easy and relaxed environment for them to be in, and how you get something good to eat on the table. Obviously you will want to offer your guests some delicious food, but you don't have to be a 'great cook' in order for people to have a good time in your house. There's always room for some culinary trickery, whether it is laying a beautiful tray at teatime or getting breakfast ready.

My main advice is this: keep it simple. Don't do five different vegetables because it's very difficult to have them all ready at the same time. Learn how to cook the perfect roast chicken in a style that suits the season and the occasion – roast chicken is a personal favourite of mine and a culinary confidence builder. Discover something you are happy to cook over and over again, and you'll find that the more you cook it the better you get. Who wants to start learning how to cook something new an hour before six people are arriving at your house for dinner? Learn how to shop – this is as simple as taking advice from your butcher, fishmonger, wine merchant and greengrocer – and buy good produce in season. Don't be afraid to cheat and buy pre-prepared dishes, but learn how to mix them in with other things that you have cooked.

The way you serve your guests tells them as much about how pleased you are to see them as the number of hours you've spent in the kitchen. Culinary trickery is partly about finding special treats, how you present and serve things, shopping and styling – and a little bit of cooking. Don't bother to use the oven if all a beautiful dessert or salad requires is clever arranging. Entertaining is as much about your home and the environment you create as the food you cook, and while what you provide must taste good, you don't necessarily have to have struggled over a hot oven in order to put something on the table.

While abundance is important, it can be a little overwhelming. I remember as a child going to visit my mother's friend Marge. She is a woman of enormous style and a fabulous cook. I cannot remember a single meal that she cooked, but I do remember the small glass plates of figs that she once served at the end of dinner and how enticing they looked, much more so than an overflowing fruit bowl dumped on the table. If your produce is good it will sell itself, so let it. Allow food to be its simple, glorious self and oddly enough people will think you're terribly clever, when all you did was choose a pretty plate and an unexpected time to serve it. Amazing isn't it?

I hope you enjoy this book and it inspires you to invite people over for supper or to visit for the weekend.

Rita x.

GATHERING
PEOPLE

GATHERING PEOPLE

Inviting people to your home is not difficult at all and shouldn't be the least bit frightening. If the thought of a dinner party makes you nervous, try to think of it as simply having people over for supper – that's all it really is. I still get nervous sometimes, especially when I invite someone I don't know terribly well. There are always a few insecure moments when I worry they will think I'm weird, and I have to try to remember the last time I thought someone I didn't know very well was a freak for inviting me to their house. That is a good test – I'm always flattered and excited to be asked somewhere new. Always invite new people you like, mixed in with old friends you think they might get along with. There are people who champion themselves as heroes for just throwing people together and letting them get on with it. While this can be a marvellous thing, mostly it isn't. I find you do have to think about your guests more than that.

The only thing to fear is the silent table – and I think this only happens if you invite a bunch of people who have nothing to say to each other. There are also people who gather 'interesting' people, like trophies of their amazing social skills. A room full of these 'interesting' people can be hellish. They do not always find one another interesting and you can end up with too many big characters together. You need listeners as well as talkers at any table. When you think about your friends and acquaintances, consider their characters and not necessarily their careers. After 7 p.m. people generally don't want to be judged by their work. I certainly don't.

When you invite people to your house you can control what you serve and how, but you can never know how your guests will interact or behave once you put them together. So don't feel that it's all your responsibility to make it a marvellous occasion. It won't always be, and it isn't always necessary that it should be. Sometimes it's enough to have made everyone feel welcome in your home. If you relax and let things take their course, there's a pretty good chance of the party being fun for you and everyone else. A friend of mine once came to a dinner party at my house with her own steak and chips takeaway! Remain calm in these situations. One option is to get upset about it, but the preferable one is to stick the takeaway in the oven to keep warm and get on with the evening. I would like to add that this incident had more to do with my friend's own dietary weirdness than my cooking.

INVITATIONS

It is worth being very clear when you invite people that you really are expecting them to come. I have just ordered some 'At Home' cards. I know that this is a faintly ridiculous thing to have done, but it was, of course, the faint ridiculousness that appealed to me. I was ordering writing paper and got carried away. These cards are not the usual black and white cards with fancy script but pale green, with simple scarlet writing saying 'Rita at Home'. I am delighted with them and I love sending them out. They set a date in stone and they give you an opportunity to say whatever you want to about your dinner – what time, where and what the occasion is – should you want to. I like this part – it is fun to say that you are celebrating the first day of autumn or are having a dinner for a friend or whatever. 'At Home' cards may not be up your alley, but you can send out note cards or postcards to invite people. There is plenty of pretty stationery about that is ideal for this sort of thing. If you are any good at drawing, get plain cards and customise them yourself.

People love getting an invitation. You feel a bit more excited about going somewhere if you are invited by post and you want to take more time over what you are going to wear. Invitations don't have to be stuffy and you can invite people by telephone so you get a response immediately, then send the invitation to confirm. When you invite by post only, you have to wait for your friends to get the invitation and then reply. It doesn't give you much time to invite other people when you get some refusals. I find that if I don't confirm, by phone or post, I am highly likely to lose a few guests. You can also say things like, 'please make sure that all cancellations come 24 hours before the dinner'. I know that sounds a bit ridiculous, but cancellations have become a real bugbear for me, and they generally come from people who have only ever accepted hospitality, never offered it.

If you are inviting people to stay for a weekend or longer, I recommend that you send a letter to confirm when you are expecting them to arrive and when you are expecting them to leave. When an invitation is written down like this it lets people know you are serious and that they are really expected to arrive.

RSVP

If someone asks you to come to something, you have to respond. No exceptions. Personally, I don't care if someone comes or not. I just want to know, because if they can't I would like to ask someone else. I would much rather someone turned down my invitation than kept me waiting in case something better comes along. Never chase an RSVP. Take silence as a rather rude way of saying that they can't come, put them on the back burner for the next thing, and invite someone else. If they then reply at the last minute, say that you are very sorry but you assumed, since it took them four days to work out what they were doing for supper next Wednesday, they couldn't come. They will get a bit of a shock and won't wait so long next time. There are far too many nice people who would love to come for supper to worry about the ones who are skitting about the place waiting to see what else might come along.

And who else is coming?

Whether it is rude or not to ask who's coming to dinner seems to be a constant question. While I don't want to start pontificating on manners I would like to touch on this subject, partly because I don't think that there is a straight answer. Obviously, it is monstrously rude to ask before you have accepted or declined, but after that it becomes a bit of a grey area. I think that sometimes when you are inviting someone that you don't know very well it's nice to give them an idea of who else is coming, just to put them at ease. There may be a couple of people who you know they know too.

But on the whole, I think it's best not to tell people who's coming, simply because the guest list is one of your major trump cards of the evening. It's like knowing what is in a parcel before you unwrap it. As a guest, it's much more fun to go to dinner not knowing who is going to be there.

ARRIVING AND LEAVING

Again, I don't want to get to stuck on anything that is going to start being seen as etiquette, but this is a question that has been put to me. Arrive when you have been asked to, but you aren't usually expected to get there on the dot. The general rule is to arrive 15 minutes after the time you have been invited but I think anything up to half an hour after the time is fine.

I can never remember what time I have asked anyone so it never bothers me and I don't think it matters – someone has to be first, after all. What is annoying is when people are really late. If you are asked for 8.30 and you arrive at 9.30, don't expect to be asked again for a while.

Leaving is usually quite obvious. You can't really go until dinner is over, although sometimes this seems like it might be an eternity. I have sat flagging at dinners and just as I have thought it might be OK to make a move, the hostess asks if anyone wants coffee and I want to kill myself. I think once coffee has been drunk it is safe to go, but you just can't do an obvious eat and run. Also, when you leave, don't make a big song and dance about it. This is one reason why it is better to have coffee sitting on sofas – when everyone is getting up and down anyway, those who want to leave have a good opportunity to do so. Those that want to stay, but talk to someone else, can, and anyone who wants to remain sitting at the table can do that too.

IT'S ANNOYING WHEN PEOPLE ARE REALLY LATE.
IF YOU ARE ASKED FOR 8.30 AND ARRIVE AT 9.30,
DON'T EXPECT TO BE INVITED AGAIN FOR A WHILE.

HOW TO BE AN EASY GUEST

1 It is very dull to talk about journeys. Once you have arrived somewhere try to keep quiet about how long it took you to get there.

2 Try to avoid road-rage incidents on the way to friends' houses as it can be embarrassing when they walk in behind you.

3 It is very boring to ask for herbal tea when you are asked what you would like to drink on arrival. I know this sounds extraordinary, but it has become quite fashionable. It is a nightmare, though – no one wants to watch a kettle boil when they have a room full of guests.

4 It is always nice to arrive at someone's house with something (uninvited pets do not fall into this category). There are times when one wants to take a bottle of wine, but equally there are times when this is just not right at all. At those moments I usually plump for treats to have with coffee. These are always easy to buy and much appreciated, especially if they are as yet unknown to your hostess.

5 Try to leave fear at home. It can be terrifying walking into a house not knowing whether you are going to know anyone. You will always be richly rewarded for doing it, but when you look frightened or nervous it is usually mis-read as rude or hostile, which works for no one.

6 As a hostess you must try to remember to introduce people. I often forget this and then

realise at the end of dinner. It is crucial and so easily forgotten. And use people's full names: it is really so tiresome this business of being informal and just using first names because it means that you leave places not really feeling sure about who anyone was.

7 When you are introducing yourself it is important to use your whole name too. It is just so annoying when someone says, 'Hi, I'm Carl.' Carl who? You have no idea about them with that sort of information. Be proud of your name, it is your identity. I am guilty of failing to give my whole name sometimes, but I am getting better. People will remember you if you use your name in full.

8 If you are going to be the first to leave then don't make a song and dance about it. Try to be discreet: don't announce it loudly and then go around the entire table saying goodbye. It is really tedious for everyone.

9 When you decide to leave, leave quickly. There is nothing duller for a hostess than standing around for half an hour saying goodbye to someone. Stay and chat or get up and go, but being a straggling leaver is like some weird form of attention seeking.

10 Never get up and offer to help your hostess clear up. If you really care, then you can stay with her after everyone has gone. There is nothing nicer than one or two lingering for a last glass and a gossip.

ETIQUETTE

The first thing that I would like to say about etiquette is that the word alone makes the hairs on the back of my neck stand on end. I think the whole business is pretty awful and dates back to a time when there was a much more rigid social structure than there is now. Unless you are going to Buckingham Palace I wouldn't give etiquette too much thought.

What does matter is manners. These are really designed to keep everyone happy and without them, you just end up upsetting people. Everyone has different views, but there are only two things I care about.

First, I really cannot bear mobile phones on the table. It is a totally unacceptable habit and I wish that it was so obvious that it wouldn't be worth mentioning, but it happens all the time. To any friends of mine who are guilty of this – be embarrassed, because I mean it, and every one of you is lucky that my editor thought a list of your names was going too far! Turn your phone off or put it on to silent (that includes disabling the vibrating ring) when you arrive in someone's house. I don't know how to make it any clearer than that – it is just exceptionally rude. This applies whether you are at a kitchen supper for two or a party of 12.

Second, I am not wild about small children and babies at dinner. I love them all through the day, but after 8 o'clock I want to be able to have grown-up conversation, uninterrupted by 'why's' and crying, and I want to be able to swear at liberty just like the BBC.

So those are my two things and I hope they don't make me sound too dragony or snotty.

COMMITMENT

I can't bear people cancelling dinner at the last minute and I really mind when it's on the day itself. Cancelling at the last minute shows no consideration for you or for the effort that goes into getting dinner together. I do think that 24 hours' notice is necessary. When people cancel or forget an invitation it is insulting and I think you can say so. But this is easier said than done. We are all so concerned about not being uptight that we let these things go and accept quite awful behaviour. I am terrified of people thinking I'm uptight and I always say that it doesn't matter – even though it does. But I do make a mental note and I don't bother inviting them again for a while. If they make a habit of cancelling, they soon drop off the end of the list. You can't conduct a friendship with somebody who lets you down all the time.

FIRST TIMERS

When I'm inviting someone I don't know very well to my house for the first time, I can get anxious about who they are going to like. Inviting other people your guest knows makes things easier, and you can usually find at least one person you know in common. In trundling along this route, though, I have found myself in danger of having eight people in my house, none of whom I know terribly well. This is slightly dodgy ground. You need some allies at a party if you are to be a comfortable and relaxed hostess. Combine new and old, and try my old favourite, the daisy-chain effect: make sure everyone knows someone, while there is no one who knows either everyone or no one.

FRIEND THIEVING

Some people are very happy to introduce you to their friends but don't much like it when you become friends with them yourself. This is not something I've ever minded, but you need to be aware of it. It's no good upsetting one friend to make another. Don't feel you have to forfeit the new friend, but be sensitive in the way you do things, involving your old friend along the way.

If you meet people at dinner it can feel slightly embarrassing and gauche to ask for their number at the end of that first evening. So what should you do? Stay calm; nothing has to be done immediately. When you call to thank your friend for dinner, mention how much you enjoyed meeting Bill and Ted. Ask for their number, saying how much you would like to see them again. Alternatively, next time you want to have people over, invite your hostess. When she accepts, ask for Bill and Ted's number, explaining that you would like to ask them too. This way you have made her a part of your new friendship.

INTRODUCTIONS

When you're busy getting dinner ready, it's very easy to forget to introduce people to one another. I did exactly this the other day. I was so absorbed in making my salad that I failed to realise that the reason one of my friends was lurking nearby in the kitchen was because he didn't know anyone sitting next door. It is terrifying for guests to walk into a room full of people they don't know but who all know one another and are gaily chatting away. Just because someone knows you and your house intimately does not mean that they know the people you have chosen to come to dinner that night. You have an obligation as hostess to make certain that everybody is introduced, and if you think they have a common interest, to offer it up.

This goes for bigger parties too. It's a common complaint that hosts no longer introduce people. This is quite a skill: it can be very tedious when you're in the middle of a discussion with a friend and some nightmarishly bossy hostess comes up and drags you off to introduce you to someone you have no interest in meeting – and they probably have none in you. There's nothing wrong with letting guests chat to people they know, and when you are introducing people you should consider whether they would be interested in one another rather than just seeing one person standing alone and grabbing someone else to talk to them. Having said that, there have been times when I have walked into a room not knowing a soul and been immensely grateful to the hostess, who welcomed me with open arms and took me around the room to introduce me to everyone.

FORMAL OR INFORMAL

If there are just a few of you for dinner, I think the nicest thing is to have people sitting around the kitchen table while you prepare the food. They can have a glass of wine, share good chatter and gobble the odd treat you sling their way to keep the wolf from the door. A little plate of good salami and gherkins, some taramasalata and toast – nibbly bits that can sit in the

You have an obligation as hostess to make certain that everyone is introduced.

middle of the table and be picked at. These are the sorts of things you can throw together while you're getting the rest of dinner ready. Another good idea is to serve mini-popadums with raita or tsatziki – all available in supermarkets and welcomed by the peckish guest.

I hate staying in the kitchen preparing food while everyone else perches politely in my sitting room, having a drink and waiting for me to come out and announce that dinner is ready. I always feel so silly going through to ask everyone to come and eat. It's far too formal. But this is a personal view. Some people like to be left alone in the kitchen.

Having everything prepared in advance of friends' arrival is another way to avoid the more formal scenario of cook in the kitchen and guests on the sofa. And it is extremely nice to sit and have a drink with your friends before dinner. Unwanted formality can come when you are over-prepared, though, as pointed out to me by my friend William the other day. He had been to dinner with me on two occasions, quite close together. The first evening I wasn't at all ready. I was running late and hurrying to get everything into some sort of pan or other. As everyone arrived they sat round the table while I cooked. The table wasn't laid and eventually I gave them some plates and cutlery and together they laid the table before we sat down to eat. My guests didn't know each other terribly well and without realising it, everyone getting involved broke the ice very easily. You would have thought they had all known each other forever by the time we sat down.

The next time William came, I was much better

organised and I'd laid the table before anyone arrived. From the start, the dinner took on a more formal atmosphere and no one came near the table until dinner was ready, leaving me alone in the kitchen. While the table looked utterly lovely, its perfection didn't entice anyone to come near – they stayed away and sat next door. But in the great scheme of things it doesn't much matter which way you do things as long as there is plenty of chatter. At the end of this particular dinner the tablecloth was suitably mucky, which is always a pretty reliable indication of a good time having been had.

It is worth remembering, though, when you are thinking about what sort of evening you intend to have, that when people get involved they instantly feel more relaxed, rather than a part in your tableau of the perfect dinner. It's not that one is right and the other is wrong, but it is worth knowing what sort of evening you are aiming for before you start.

A FEW FRIENDS OVER FOR SUPPER EARLY IN THE WEEK

The best way to handle this sort of evening is to prepare beforehand but this can be difficult, especially when you don't get home until 6 or 7 at night. There are certain things that are easy to prepare in advance and others that need little attention once they are in the oven so you are free to sit down with a glass of wine in your hand. Baked potatoes or pasta, for example, are just the sort of thing that you want to be eating on a Tuesday night with a couple of friends. I love these small, cosy dinners, which allow you to be very relaxed.

A LARGE BOWL OF PASTA IS PERFECT FOR AN INFORMAL DINNER WITH A FEW PEOPLE.

Baked potatoes

There is a trick, as with everything – stick a metal skewer through the potatoes. This makes sure they are fluffy in the middle. Prick the outsides, rub them with olive oil and salt and bung them in the oven for about an hour. The only problem is remembering to put them in the oven an hour before you want to eat them. The longer you leave them, the crispier their skins will go.

Baked potatoes can be the cornerstone of your meal. I love them with cold roast beef or ham and salad: absolutely no cooking required. You can buy the cold roast beef and/or ham from the butcher or deli and all you need to do is make sure you have excellent condiments, such as horseradish for the beef, and mustard and chutney for the ham. Beet and horseradish is particularly yummy and perfect for these sorts of dinners. You can also add something like a good French bean salad, which is very easy. Just cook some beans, thinly slice a shallot or a little red onion, and dress with some lemon, olive oil and salt while the beans are still warm.

The only time I don't enjoy baked potatoes is with stew. I am not keen on stew full stop, but I really don't like soggy-with-gravy baked potatoes. My heart sinks when I go to someone's house and they have made stew for dinner. It is just so heavy at night – it is really only suitable when the weather is extremely cold. The other thing I hate is that a stew is often a cover-up operation for the nastiest, gristliest bits of meat.

Pasta

A large bowl of pasta is perfect for an informal dinner with a few people. I would never serve pasta for more than about four because you would need such a large pan. Pasta only takes about ten minutes to cook if it is dried and two minutes if it is fresh, so there isn't much to do in advance. But in order to make it delicious there are a couple of points to bear in mind. Never buy the jars of ready-made tomato sauce in the supermarket. You can get away with pesto, but make sure you buy an Italian brand. Tomato sauce is best bought from a deli counter or made at home. It isn't difficult at all.

TOMATO SAUCE

Always have some tins of peeled Italian tomatoes in your cupboard. To make a sauce, chop half an onion and put it in a pan with a bit of garlic and olive oil. Cook until the onion is soft, add a tin or two of tomatoes and let them cook and cook and cook. Add salt and pepper. If you have a tin of anchovies, adding one or two to the pan makes the sauce rather tasty.

To cook the pasta, fill a large pan with water and add some salt and a bit of olive oil. There should be a lot more water than pasta so that the pasta can move about and doesn't get stuck together. When the water is boiling, add the pasta and reduce the heat slightly so the water stays at a simmer. The best way to know whether the pasta is cooked or not is to keep tasting it. Or if you cut one bit in half you can see very easily whether it is still hard. When the pasta is cooked, add the sauce and some mozzarella cheese cut into small pieces. It will melt and be utterly yummy. Alternatively, do what a lot of Italians do and add a spoonful or two of double cream. Mix everything together in the big pasta pan and transfer it to a large serving bowl – make sure you warm it first. Add some fresh basil at this point, too.

Serving pasta

Pasta is best eaten out of bowls. Use soup plates if you have them or large shallow bowls. There are plenty on the market. I like to put a nice piece of Parmesan cheese on the table with a grater, but there is nothing wrong with having a bowl of it already grated. The only drawback is that if you do too much it won't last long after dinner if it's not eaten, and if the bowl of cheese is finished you probably were a bit mean with it. It's always nicer to have more than is needed or people get nervous about how much to take – never a good thing.

Make a salad and serve it with the pasta or bring it to the table when everyone has finished. I wouldn't bother to serve cheese because you will have had quite enough with the pasta.

Salad dressings

I am the worst person at making salad dressings. They are either too oily or too sharp. I used to get around this by commandeering a guest to make the dressing, but I have now worked it out. It does not involve a jam jar and a list of ingredients but is simply this: splash some olive oil and balsamic vinegar over your salad, then generously sprinkle on Maldon salt and grind some black pepper. Adding salt and pepper changes the balance, so you should add salt and pepper while you are still making the dressing rather than at the end without tasting it again. You can replace balsamic vinegar with lemon juice, which is delicious and some people prefer it. Indeed, if you are dieting lemon is a better option, as balsamic vinegar contains lots of sugar.

Be careful of putting too much of anything on the salad or it will become soggy. Go gently – you can always add but you can't take away.

Tossing

Toss salad with your hands. You have far more control over it this way than with salad servers, which will always leave quite a lot of the salad on the counter. I watched a wonderful cook tossing salad with her hands in an oversized salad bowl and that is what I now do.

IT IS WORTH REMEMBERING, WHEN YOU ARE THINKING ABOUT WHAT SORT OF EVENING YOU INTEND TO HAVE, THAT WHEN PEOPLE GET INVOLVED THEY FEEL INSTANTLY MORE RELAXED, RATHER THAN A PART IN YOUR TABLEAU OF THE PERFECT DINNER.

The oversized bowl is also a good trick. Those awful little wooden bowls from kitchens of the seventies and eighties are a waste of time.

Another good idea is to prepare and toss the salad in any old big bowl and then serve it piled high on a platter. Salad served on big serving plates is really lovely and looks much better than it does in bowls. If you don't have a big enough bowl for tossing, mix the salad in the sink. Most people look at me in horror when I suggest this because they think it is unhygienic in some way. I don't understand why, as you wash the salad in the sink.

LUNCH WITH A GIRLFRIEND AT HOME

Usually you think of a gossipy lunch with a girlfriend as taking place in a restaurant, but think again. It's lovely to be at home, because you rarely get a chance to enjoy your house during the day in this way and it gives you a fabulous sense of being someone who doesn't work. The more time you can spend in your home in a leisurely fashion, the more you will love it – and I don't think that we do it enough. This lunch is probably at the weekend, giving you the morning to prepare something calmly and an ideal chance to try things out before you go on to more daunting dinner parties. You will gain confidence by doing this – first, because your girlfriend is not scary so you will be relaxed, and second, because you are catering for two people which is quite a different operation to feeding six or eight. Another great pleasure about cooking for two is that you can be a little more extravagant with the produce

The more time you spend in your home in a leisurely fashion, the more you will love it – and I don't think that we do it enough.

and you have time to do pretty things, like decant the wine into something beautiful.

Now, if you are near a good deli or traiteur there is absolutely nothing wrong with going to see what they have on offer – perhaps a little aubergine salad or delicious matoubal (Lebanese aubergine dip), roasted vegetables, all the things that fill me with horror at the idea of having to cook myself. Weekends bring such delights as farmers' markets and they are definitely worth going to for fresh produce. Buy some fish or meat and a good loaf of bread. A fishmonger might have dressed crab or potted shrimps – food that is ready to eat. But a piece of fish is extremely easy to cook if you simply wrap it in a piece of foil with some lemon and olive oil. I don't really recommend having more than one thing that you have to cook from a recipe. It just gets too complicated and you want to be chatting to your friend, not kneeling with your head in the oven.

Pick up a bunch of flowers at the market if there are any, and buy a good bottle of wine. Once you are home with your shopping you can set about the trickery. The salads from the deli go on to beautiful plates and the cartons straight in the bin. This leaves you with only one thing to cook, which you can do very calmly. I would suggest looking in one of the many cookery books I bet you have and finding something simple. Simple is always good.

The other bonus about entertaining girlfriends is that they will appreciate the effort of a beautifully laid table and they will sit there happily with a glass of wine while you put the final touches to lunch.

The plough girl's lunch

This involves hardly any cooking, just clever shopping for food such as cheddar and good chutney. This lunch could be boring, but if you shop well it will be delicious. A truckle of cheddar will make your table look really pretty and you can serve it with some delicious oatcakes, the rougher the better, which you can find in swanky delis or good farm shops. Once you start thinking of cooking in terms of shopping you will find that, whenever you see them, you start picking up things like good oatcakes and chutneys, and then you can keep them at the ready.

ONCE YOU START COOKING IN TERMS OF SHOPPING YOU WILL FIND THAT, WHENEVER YOU SEE THEM, YOU START PICKING UP THINGS SUCH AS GOOD OATCAKES AND CHUTNEYS, AND THEN YOU CAN KEEP THEM AT THE READY.

Salade Niçoise

Salade Niçoise is a good thing to serve for lunch and there is a cool way of making it look stylish, which I pinched from my friends Neil and Amelia. When I lunched with them on their roof terrace in New York, they served a niçoise with all the ingredients arranged separately on a beautiful long platter, instead of being mixed together as usual. This is the ultimate in culinary trickery because there is really nothing to this salad except style.

The traditional ingredients are lettuce, tomatoes, French beans, tuna, onion, peppers, radishes, new potatoes, anchovies and olives. You can make it with all or some of those ingredients, depending on what you like.

I hate black olives in salade Niçoise; Atkinsers don't like the potatoes. Many people don't like anchovies, but if you can get to a deli that sells the white ones you'll find they are much less hardcore than the brown tinned ones. If you can cope, get fresh tuna and sear it yourself. Otherwise I don't think anyone will be too horrified if you use a tin, but make sure it is a good brand. Squeeze some lemon over the tuna and add some black pepper. It's also vital to put a fork through it so that it isn't a little round thing with the can marks imprinted on it – I am sure you wouldn't do this, but I don't want to take any chances. Then hard-boil a few eggs. Delia knows how to do this very well and details are overleaf.

SALADE NIÇOISE IS A GOOD THING TO SERVE FOR LUNCH AND THIS IS A COOL WAY OF MAKING IT LOOK STYLISH.

QUICK LESSON IN MAKING HARD-BOILED EGGS

Put the eggs in a pan of cold water so they are covered, bring up to a simmer and time them for six minutes. Delia has a great tip to stop the yolks going blue like those filthy ones you used to get at school: you must cool them or they continue cooking and that is when they go blue. It is also impossible to peel an egg that is hot. I usually put them in a bowl under the cold tap. I then crack the shell all over and peel under the running tap so that the water washes the bits of shell away. Some people say that you should peel from the bottom of the egg.

Back to the salad

The tomatoes should be peeled, too, and this is very easy to do. Pop them into a pan of boiling water for a minute, then test them by piercing the skin with a knife. If the skin falls away, take the tomatoes out and they will be easy to peel. Use plum or beef tomatoes and cut them into quarters or strips, depending on how you want your salad to look, I like either chunky or strips – no dicing! Use only the heart of the lettuce – those limp, dark outer leaves are just too depressing and you can never get them on to your fork. I love round lettuce, but there is no reason why you shouldn't use baby gems or romaine if you want to. And finally the onion: I would thinly slice shallots or chop a red onion – or you could go off-recipe and use spring onion. This is all about presentation, so pile the ingredients on your dish and your lunch is done.

Dressing

The dressing is a bit of a problem with this style of salad. I'm usually pretty insistent that all salads must be served already dressed and tossed, but there are exceptions to all rules, even one's own. You can put a jug of French dressing on the table and let each person dress her own salad. Alternatively, when you're ready to eat, pour the dressing over the salad and toss it at the table. But for this salad, the bonus of leaving it for everyone to help themselves and dress their own is that they can leave the bits of the niçoise they don't like.

I'M USUALLY PRETTY INSISTENT THAT ALL SALADS MUST BE SERVED READY DRESSED AND TOSSED, BUT THERE ARE EXCEPTIONS TO ALL RULES, EVEN ONE'S OWN.

SUNDAY EVENING

This is a nice time to have a friend over. A lot of people would disagree, but I love anything that distracts me from the fact that it is Monday in the morning. I don't think this is a good time for anything too major, though, as you are probably quite tired. Keep it to two of you – possibly a telly supper. I love eating curry on a Sunday night and this only requires picking up the telephone. Ideally what you want for telly suppers is something that requires no cutting up and can be eaten from a bowl. A delicious risotto is perfect, if you can face the stirring. I would avoid pasta because if you are anything like me you will have overeaten during the weekend and so it's best not to add to the discomfort by eating a bowl of such major carbs. Somehow I don't think risotto is quite so bad.

Mushrooms on toast

These are a treat, and in the autumn it is easy to come by excellent wild mushrooms. Buy chanterelles and fry them up with some olive oil, garlic, onion, salt and pepper, or bake the larger types of mushrooms with a bit of crushed garlic and pop them on some toast. If you have some cheese, add a slice on top of the mushrooms and put the whole thing under the grill. This will, of course, need cutting up unless you eat it with your hands, but it's not so difficult. You could cut the toast into squares before you put the mushrooms on top.

Potted shrimps

Potted shrimps are so good. Buy when you can and put them in the freezer to bring out when you want. The best thing with potted shrimps is brown toast – it doesn't matter if it gets cold before you eat it. I love cold toast and butter, as long as it isn't soggy. NEVER, never pile toast – if it is piled the steam rises and the toast goes soggy, which is most disagreeable. Always put toast in a rack or stand it up. I also think you should trim off the crusts and cut it into triangles or small squares for serving with potted shrimps. Cut some wedges of lemon and off you go. Don't plate this supper. Just put the lemon wedges and the toast in the middle of the table for people to help themselves from. I hate portion control and this way looks and feels more generous.

NEVER, never pile toast – if it is piled the steam rises and the toast goes soggy, which is most disagreeable. Always put toast in a rack or stand it up.

I LOVE EATING CURRY ON A SUNDAY NIGHT AND THIS ONLY REQUIRES PICKING UP THE TELEPHONE.

Ready-made meals

I don't recommend buying too many ready-made foods from around the world in the supermarket. If you do, you need to be careful in your choices. My friends Eck and Lucy and I recently had a Chinese Sunday night supper entirely from the supermarket. The first problem was that we bought too many different things, which is always a risk with Chinese food anyway. I got confused about heating times – what went in for ten minutes, 15 or 25; what needed just the top searing and what had to be removed from its packet. Of course, I melted most of the containers and it was disgusting.

If you buy ready-prepared stuff, buy at the top of the market, which in supermarket terms is generally affordable. Don't buy too many things because, unless I am especially thick, like me you'll find it becomes a hideous maths problem working out all the different cooking times. Stick to uncomplicated dishes. Curry is generally good, because it is something that was designed to be cooked the day before anyway, but cook your own rice. It's not that difficult. If you do want to buy ready-made rice, make sure it's plain. Take care in the Chinese section. Crispy duck and pancakes are generally safe, but the rice is gross and tastes like school rice with peas and sweet corn. Anything with a glupey sauce is not only going to be disgusting but will also be packed with sugar and spend the next few months settling itself on your bottom.

Basically I would say that ready-made meals are a big NO. I have been sent many by companies who claim to be the new smart-ready-made-meal people.

They want me to try their meals and write about them, but luckily for the companies, I have tried them and not written about them. If you want something quick, there's corn on the cob – how delicious, how uncomplicated and how good for you.

Omelette and salad

Another Sunday night option I like is an omelette and salad. This is greatly improved by a bottle of red wine and, for this sort of occasion where you may not want to drink much, I love a half bottle. It is just so civilised. Somehow I feel that one always wants a bit of linen somewhere near a half bottle of claret. Have a very large, starched linen napkin if your plate is on your lap, or if you prefer to sit at a table for your telly supper, put a small cloth over a card table and sit there. Lay the table beautifully for your omelette and salad dinner and it becomes something rather lovely and so much more special than an omelette eaten off a kitchen plate on your knees. I love simple dishes like this combined with the luxury of linen and a good glass of wine.

I LOVE SIMPLE DISHES . . . COMBINED WITH THE LUXURY OF LINEN AND A GOOD GLASS OF WINE.

If you are a regular dinner-for-two person it's great to make this a special event. For example, if you and your husband, boyfriend, girlfriend or whatever have supper together every Sunday, make it a lovely ritual and buy good china and glass – you only need two of everything.

Baked eggs

Easy and delicious, these are perfect Sunday evening fare and are even good for children's tea. Baked eggs also make a good first course – if you're into doing first courses, which I'm not because it tends to leave everything else in a slight state of chaos. You can vary this dish by what you put under the eggs. For example, chop up some mushrooms and fry them in a pan with a little butter or olive oil and maybe salt and pepper. Put them in the bottom of a ramekin dish, break an egg over the top, add a slug of cream, season and pop it in the oven. Cooking time depends on how soft you like the yolk. My granny used to have gold ramekins, which were rather snappy. They're not produced now, but would be lovely for jazzing up baked eggs; keep an eye out for them in antiques shops and markets.

Mark Birley, founder of Annabel's Club in London, highly recommends cracked eggs – baked eggs in tomato sauce. Take some little baking dishes (like the ones for serving individual lasagnes in Italian restaurants), pour in some tomato sauce, then crack an egg into the middle. Pop into a preheated oven for about ten minutes.

ENTERTAINING IN-LAWS OR OTHER VIPS

Because you want to make a good impression and have the evening go well, you can get nervous, and this can be fatal. If you think it would help, there's nothing wrong with diluting in-laws with some other people. Adding a couple of friends into the mix often takes the pressure off you.

This is the one time that you absolutely MUST NOT try a new recipe. Cook something you know how to do well and if you don't know anything, follow my suggestions below. Or simply roast a chicken (see pages 142–3). As long as it is cooked through, you can't go wrong. If you take the chicken out of the oven and find the legs are still quite pink, don't panic; the rest will probably be cooked to perfection. Just cut the legs off, chuck them back in the oven and bring them out for seconds. Cook the chicken upside down to keep it juicy.

> There's nothing wrong with diluting the in-laws with some other people. Adding a couple of friends into the mix often takes the pressure off you.

Rack of lamb

This cut cooks itself beautifully and you then carve it into separate cutlets, which look very elegant. Your in-laws will never know you haven't got a clue about what you're doing in the kitchen, although you don't want to cook this for more than four to six people. Allow two or three cutlets for women and three or four for men. Ask the butcher to prepare the rack for you. He will cut the fat from the bone so that once the meat is cooked and cut up you can hold the cutlets in your fingers, which you definitely should do when it's all getting too fancy.

When you get back from the butcher, get out a

large bowl and pour in some olive oil and add about three crushed cloves of garlic. Take some sprigs of rosemary and pull the leaves off the branch into the olive oil. If you have a pestle and mortar, crush the garlic, rosemary and salt together to release more flavour. Put the meat into the bowl and turn until it is coated in the scented oil, cover with a cloth and leave it for as long as you can – at least a couple of hours. If you are cooking for four and have two racks you might need two bowls of oil.

When you're ready to cook the meat, remove it from the oil, place in a roasting tin and put into a hot (preheated) oven for about 20 minutes. I like lamb pink. If you don't, leave the racks in a little longer. Check by cutting it in the middle, as that is where it will be rarest. Once the meat is cooked to your liking, let it rest for about ten minutes before carving.

Vegetables

While the meat is resting, cook your vegetables if you are just doing boiled or steamed. Your options are endless – go to A thing or two about vegetables (pages 154–5) and choose what you want. You could add a roasted vegetable if you think it necessary or on a winter's evening, a flavoured mash (see page 150) would be good. Both will take longer than ten minutes so don't wait for the meat to be resting before you start. In the summer, try asparagus or some chopped runner beans with a little flat-leaf parsley for a little extra flavour.

Rocket salad

Rocket salad with some shaved Parmesan on the top is

delicious with lamb. You may find you need to trim the rocket leaves, as they can be stalky and too long; this takes time but it is worth it.

Cheese

The rack of lamb is a perfect dinner and extremely easy. But if you are worried about whether you are serving enough, have a cheese course. This will help the men along if they didn't get enough of the main course, and cheese and salad only really works when everyone has a little space left. If you are having cheese, serve the salad with it instead of with the lamb, and a baguette or some oatcakes. I would go for the roughest oatcakes you can find. For more on cheese see pages 156–7.

Thai trickery

Another option for dinner with the in-laws is to serve a Thai green curry. Just pick it up from your local Thai restaurant on the way home and don't tell a soul. I have done this before and I don't think there is anything wrong with it. No one is going to make green curry better than a Thai person anyway, and curry is one thing that travels really well. If your local happens to be an Indian, do that instead. But if you are to pull this off, don't buy anything else. I mean it. When you get home, decant the curry into a large pan, the sort that you might use for making curry. Dispose of the foil evidence and take the rubbish out. Heat the curry up in the pan and cook your own rice and some broccoli with oyster sauce. If anyone asks questions, just say that the curry is really easy to make, which I've heard it is anyway. If your mother-in-law is vulgar enough to ask you for the recipe, say that Li, your Thai friend, gave it to you on condition that you never handed it on. I know that serving your mother-in-law food from a takeaway sounds like asking for trouble, especially when you first meet her, but she is there to meet you, not sample your cooking. I know that I'm not always seen as the modern voice for women, but I would not expect any woman to judge me on my cooking skills, and certainly not because she was checking out how well I could look after her son! Don't get intimidated by the M-I-L stereotype. Knowing how to cook doesn't matter – you just need to know how to shop. Get something delicious on the table. Your choice of route is irrelevant.

WHAT OTHERS CAN BRING TO THE PARTY

If people offer to bring something to dinner I do think it is a good idea to accept. The first time this happened to me was when I invited my friend Lyn to dinner and she asked if she could bring pudding. My instinct was to say no. After all, surely it is the hostess who should provide so the guests can enjoy themselves. But something stopped me, and I said that would be lovely. Lyn and Christophe arrived, carrying a big white box of treats from a wonderful deli. I didn't know Lyn very well then and for some reason her arriving with her white box felt good and made her part of things. Giving and receiving is what it's all about. It is good to accept people's offers and it's worth remembering that when people offer to do something, it's usually because they want to. My friend Lucy always offers to bring some lettuces or herbs and it's lovely when she arrives with a beautiful basket packed with goodies. Also, on a more practical level, it gives you one less thing to think about.

There are also potluck suppers, when everyone brings a course. I have always thought of those dinners as a bit like those drawing games we used to play as children, when one person does the head and another the body and so on. Then you laugh a lot when the peculiar person is revealed. But I do think a potluck supper can be very jolly and people usually think very carefully about what they are going to make. And there is generally a healthy atmosphere of competition, which always gets people going. If you are really clever you can get enough people to bring something so all you have to do is make the coffee – and no one will notice.

When my friends Peter and Sebastian have friends to stay for the weekend they always get their guests to cook dinner on Saturday. This is a good idea for two reasons: first, it takes the pressure off the hosts for one meal – which is welcome, as you can start to feel like the hired help in your own home sometimes – and second, it gets everyone involved. There is a very relaxed atmosphere in their house and the weekend seems to be geared mostly towards cooking and eating anyway, so it works well.

Sharing know-how

The sharing of things is not only in the actual produce but also in the know-how. The best way to learn anything to do with cooking is to ask someone else – generally a lot easier than working it out from a book. My friend Lucy is great for this, and I wish I could publish her telephone number so that you, too, could call her ten minutes before your guests arrive to find out what you are meant to do with a rib roll of beef. I will try to pass on as much of her useful information as I can, but there will be bits I miss so I highly recommend that you find a Lucy of your own. This is the sort of resource pooling that is really useful and it doesn't have to stop at cooking. Share your knowledge of good shops, culinary tricks and good treats. After all, what goes around comes around, and there is really nothing worse than people who are reluctant to give out information.

Most people know how to cook one thing really well so it's worth asking them how they do it. Usually people who only know how to make one thing are happy to share their knowledge. After all, they will not really be great cooks, even if they make this one thing exceptionally, so they will probably be delighted that you like whatever they can do. Everyone loves to be asked for advice. It is deeply flattering. The other reason I like to ask someone rather than look in a book is that when people tell you how to do something verbally, they usually keep it short and not too complicated. I find reading instructions difficult and I think that this is the problem with cookery books. How can you be expected to remain interested for longer than three instructions? Find a friend instead.

SHARE YOUR KNOWLEDGE OF GOOD SHOPS, CULINARY TRICKS AND GOOD TREATS. AFTER ALL, WHAT GOES AROUND COMES AROUND AND THERE IS NOTHING WORSE THAN PEOPLE WHO ARE RELUCTANT TO GIVE OUT INFORMATION.

BREAKFASTS

BREAKFASTS

Any meal is a styling opportunity and, while I loathe anything that resembles a garnish (particularly on my scrambled eggs), I mind terribly about how something is presented. Breakfast is a great place to start with a little culinary trickery. Obviously you aren't going to want to take lots of trouble every morning, but there are times when it's lovely to have a very leisurely breakfast.

Breakfast should not be too complicated. No one is in the mood for a big number at this hour, so choose carefully what you want to do. This is where the trickery comes in: keep it simple, but still make it look glorious. Your approach to this meal will change depending on whether you are making breakfast for you and your boyfriend, for friends, or for children.

BREAKFAST EVERY DAY

I eat very little breakfast as a rule – and I'm sure I'm not alone – so be assured that I am not going to suggest that you make a big deal out of it every morning before you set out for work. I know that there are plenty of people who cannot operate until they have had their cup of builder's, but I am strictly a coffee person in the morning so let's start with that.

The enjoyment you get from a cup of coffee depends very much on the way that it is served. I find filter coffee in a mug slightly depressing; it simply doesn't cut the mustard. So first of all – a little shopping for china. I am a great fan of the French breakfast cup. The French really know how to do breakfast china and the marvellous thing is that you don't need very much of it. A pair of cups and beautiful plates should be enough, so you can afford to buy slightly more expensive things. A morning latte or cappuccino is easily made with the help of a few must-have items, such as a latte whisk for frothing milk. You also need a little saucepan to use with the whisk – I have a small enamel one that I love. It's good to start the day with pretty things so try to find something charming.

While an espresso machine can be very expensive, the old Italian favourite made by Bialetti is not. This is the cheapest way to make espresso coffee and it does something that the fancy espresso machines can't do – it fills your home with that unbeatable smell of freshly brewed coffee. The rest depends almost entirely on the coffee you put in the machine. I recommend Illy or Lavazza – the one that comes in the silver and red foil packets.

An alternative to big breakfast cups is the French tradition of serving coffee in a bowl; especially good for dipping your croissant in. Use the ordinary white rice bowls you can find in any of the major high street shops, or anything else that doesn't have a rim and

THE ENJOYMENT YOU GET FROM A CUP OF COFFEE DEPENDS VERY MUCH ON THE WAY THAT IT IS SERVED. I FIND FILTER COFFEE IN A MUG SLIGHTLY DEPRESSING; IT SIMPLY DOESN'T CUT THE MUSTARD.

isn't too shallow. You can find beautiful old spongeware bowls in antique shops that make perfect breakfast china. If you like your coffee short and strong, you could use the lovely little French wine tumblers that you can buy for very little money and look wonderful, especially for espresso or macchiatos. Larger tumblers are good for lattes and cappuccinos. On weekdays when I'm working, I like having my coffee in a pint glass so I search junk shops for old ones, which are large and sturdy. They're great to drink from – like having a latte grande from Starbucks, only it will taste better out of your own machine and certainly look more stylish.

If you buy small glasses for your macchiato or espresso you can also use them for orange juice, best if squeezed yourself. It's always good to have a few uses for the things you buy, otherwise you just run out of cupboard space fantastically quickly, let alone money. I like multi-functional items. They feel practical and prevent things from becoming commonplace.

LAZY SATURDAY MORNING FOR TWO

Running down to the shops for fresh croissants and the newspapers is one of the delights of Saturday mornings. If you are too far from a good patisserie there are other options. I met some people the other day who told me that they buy the best croissants in bulk and freeze them. Apparently they freeze very well. One of my friends swears by supermarket croissants and says they are properly buttery, so give them a try; you may be pleasantly surprised. An alternative to this continental start is good bread, and most of us have some sort of bakery nearby; even the local 'open all hours' shops usually have some freshly baked bread. Baguettes are delicious if you cut them into quite long pieces, slice them in half and eat them as they are or toasted under the grill briefly. Good with butter and jam, especially if you go the coffee-in-a-bowl route.

So for your breakfast tray, a plate with a couple of warm croissants or baguette is a good start, but a rack of hot toast is just as good. For the toast crowd, it is worth checking markets for old silver toast racks – piled-up toast goes soggy very quickly. If you don't have a rack, I quite like toast propped up between the jam pots. Which brings us to the jam. This benefits from being decanted unless it comes in a particularly lovely jar, which it probably

won't. Buy up little glass pots when you see them or look out for old single glasses in shops and markets – they are perfect for jam. Even those little glass yoghurt pots from France are ideal. Jam pots should not be large because they have got to be a one-hit wonder only. There is nothing more disgusting than a glass smeared with congealed jam in the fridge, except perhaps a child's face smothered in congealed egg coming towards you. I know it sounds labour intensive, but once you are on this trip, the whole point is that everything should look lovely. You can also always find odd bits of silver cutlery in junk shops and little coffee spoons are handy for jam.

Decanting milk and other dairy treats

The other thing that I love decanting is milk. Use old wine carafes or you can sometimes find old-fashioned milk bottles in kitchen shops. I have one with a cow moulded on the front. This is practical as a bottle fits in the fridge more easily than a jug, which takes up quite a lot of room. Buy a chinagraph pencil in an art shop and write the expiry date on the glass. Otherwise you just have to trust your nose!

Many people like yoghurt for breakfast. Greek yoghurt has a wonderful creamy texture but always comes in horrible plastic cartons, so definitely needs decanting into something beautiful. Use a glass bowl or shallow dish and drizzle the yoghurt with honey. Make pools in the surface with the back of a spoon first to hold the honey. (I find yoghurt needs a lot of help from honey before it becomes worth entertaining first thing in the morning; anything bitter on the palate is like taking a cold shower.) My godfather has a pot of yoghurt every morning and, while I am not a fan of natural yoghurt, his always looks very delicious. It comes in a glass pot and is served in a glass bowl packed with ice. Even though I know that it is the same sour natural yoghurt inside, it looks appealing – such is the power of presentation. The same applies to fruit: grapes in a bowl of ice look deeeeelicious, much better than an ordinary bunch sitting on a plate looking a bit dusty.

But back to the yoghurt. You can add berries or granola and you can buy good granolas in specialist delis or even at supermarkets. Once home, granola needs to be taken out of its plastic bag and kept in large glass jars. I avoid those plastic containers, which are quite ugly, and always go for glass.

You can also do your own morning pots, especially good if you are not planning on laying the table. Find a glass tumbler, quite a wide one. Put some crunchy granola in the bottom, then some honey and a dollop of yoghurt on top. It will look so fresh and delicious and all you need to do is mix it all up when you're ready to eat. Replace the honey with fruit compote or a good runny jam if you prefer. Compotes are easy to find in specialist shops and some of the swankier supermarkets or anywhere where there are homemade jams for sale. And if you really want to go to town, make your own (see page 105). It's surprisingly easy. This is a lovely way to start the day, especially if you are making breakfast for someone else. It looks like you really know what you are doing but it's just a bit of arranging.

BREAKFAST IN BED

The right linen is important for breakfast in bed and you will want large napkins, even possibly a small tablecloth. If you lay the cloth out like a picnic rug over the bed you can take the crumbs away with the breakfast with ease. I think that you want to eat breakfast in bed like a picnic rather than as if you were in hospital. As wonderful as breakfast in bed sounds, I am never terribly comfortable sitting up in bed with a tray over my knees, trapping me, and trying to cut up my breakfast, even if I have one of those trays with legs, but maybe it is just me. An alternative is to lay breakfast at a table in your bedroom. If you have a card table you can put that up, lay it with a cloth and sit at it in your nightie. This is quite an old-fashioned idea, but nice to do for someone who is ill.

Breakfast in bed is the morning equivalent to telly supper. The key to success is in the details. Having to eat your eggs without salt because the kitchen is two floors down, and you've already been up and down three times for milk and sugar and jam, rather detracts from the pleasure. If you remember to take up the papers there will be no real reason to get up until at least lunchtime – a pretty good reward for your efforts.

Breakfast in bed for guests

You will probably be quite clear in your own mind whether or not this is something you are prepared to do, and there are degrees to which you can get involved. You can take up a combination of all of the things mentioned above, but the chances are that you are not really going to want to play chambermaid to your friends. One time when breakfast is bed is a particularly good idea is for a friend who is stuck in her bedroom with a baby. Something hot upstairs will be very well received, so a complete pleasure to do. Mothers of new babies are very satisfying targets for these sorts of treats because they are generally in a state where everybody needs them and nobody is spoiling them at all. Coffee and a plate of scrambled eggs is a good thing to pop up with, or toast already buttered and jammed – remember she has only one free hand because the other one is holding the baby. I also think that when you are offering this you need to say, 'Would you prefer tea or coffee?' so that the question is much more about which one they would like rather than would they like it, and then, 'Eggs or just toast?' Then she doesn't have to think or feel like she is a burden. Someone with a baby in someone else's house is usually feeling like a burden anyway, so unless you are totally fed up already, this is a good way to look after her.

The other thing to do is to take up just tea or coffee to friends who are staying. It is lovely to be brought a cup of coffee in the morning, and it makes them feel very welcome and well looked after without the hassle of trays of food. The coffee or tea route is ideal if you have got in-laws staying or anyone you want to make feel at home. Of course, your in-laws might be the last people you want to make feel at home, but it is good to have them on side. I rather like getting a biscuit too – something very plain. It is so old-fashioned and nice.

I think you want to eat breakfast in bed like a picnic rather than as if you were in hospital.

BIG COOKED BREAKFAST DOWNSTAIRS

For anyone doing Atkins, a cooked breakfast is really the only option as carbs are hard to avoid with any of the other breakfast things. A plate of crispy bacon is yummy, especially when eaten in your fingers and accompanied by a cup of hot lemon and ginger – or as yummy as can be expected when dieting. A boiled egg is a good breakfast to have any time and you can make it look so charming. You can find eggcups in all sorts of colours and a mixture is fun to have, depending on the style route you are taking. You often see egg cups in junk shops and I love the wonderful blue and white striped kitchen china we all know so well. Buy eggcups that look good together because one egg is never enough. I like ceramic egg trays and these are the best option if you're having a big family breakfast. I also like the moulded glass eggcups from France that are shaped like hens with the eggcup bit in their backs.

Eggcups are also a lovely thing to collect and my friend Lucy says that they are the only things to buy as souvenirs. She has wooden ones from the Alps and various other places and they look adorable on the breakfast table.

Boiled eggs

Now, these eggs. I can boil six eggs to get one that is right. It is just the worst thing when you have thrown the water out and bashed the top only to find the egg white is like snot. Delia Smith is the woman who taught Britain how to get it right, so here is her method:

Put the eggs in a pan with water covering them by about half an inch. Bring to the boil, then reduce the heat so the water is simmering and leave for:

- 3 minutes for really soft eggs
- 4 minutes for the whites to be set and the yolks creamy
- 5 minutes for both the whites and the yolks to be perfectly set with the yolk only a little bit squidgy in the centre.

Boiled eggs come into their own as a meal for one and I like to lay up with little individual salt and pepper pots, toast and butter. If you have any square or oblong plates, this is the time to use them – I find that a round plate never really works for boiled eggs and toast. For Atkinsers, it's best to boil the egg for four or five minutes, and then chop it up in a small bowl with salt and pepper. This way it can be eaten with a teaspoon without noticing the absence of the soldiers too much. If you have overcooked the eggs and they are hard, chop them up, add some butter and you turn a disaster into something that tastes rather good. For children, a chopped-up egg in a small cup is very easy to eat.

Porridge

I think porridge is rather delicious and I have been eating it a lot recently. I have never been able to eat porridge made with water and seasoned with salt – far too bleak for me. I like the milk and soft brown sugar route. Porridge needs to be eaten straight from the hob.

It does not sit around well, but it can be resurrected with a jolly good stir and some hot milk.

To make porridge, pour the oats into a pan and add milk. Follow the instructions on the packet for quantities, but the oats will soak up a lot of the liquid so you must keep stirring and adding the milk as you like. I don't like porridge too runny, but it depends on your own taste. When it's done, spoon it into bowls and then top with soft brown sugar and cream if you like. I have never been brave enough to have the cream (it's a chance my hips just can't afford to take), but my friend Cathy says it is utterly delicious. In the summer, some berries over the top are good, and in winter you could add dried fruits, honey or a compote. When I was a child I liked golden syrup on my porridge (I still do).

Giant breakfast

If you have a few people to cook breakfast for, it's fun to take the largest frying pan you have and make one giant fried egg with half a dozen eggs. Put them on a large plate in the middle of the table, with bacon and maybe some sausages, so everyone can help themselves. Some fried beef tomatoes would be good as well.

The orange platter

Some friends of mine do this. It is very good breakfast and works for Sunday night, too. As you might have guessed, it is entirely orange: eggs, bacon, baked beans, fish fingers and fried bread. I have never had one – it frightens me a bit. It is the sort of thing you see people eating in the British Heart Foundation advertisements!

Bacon butties

Bacon butties, on the other hand, are one of my very favourite things and so good on a cold day. You can make them with toast or bread. Both are delicious and really good when you are outside – if you should find yourself up early at a market or camping. If you go the bread route, I suggest using thick slices of white bloomer with butter, ketchup and back bacon, the original buttie, to my mind. Any sort of bacon will do between toast. The other thing about bacon butties is that they are hard to do badly, which means you can order them anywhere and you will get something that tastes good. I think bacon butties are best with a mug of instant rather than fancy coffee. There are times when you can't beat instant, and greasy breakfast is one of them.

Egg and bacon bap

One of the best things ever for a picnic breakfast is a bacon and egg bap, wrapped in foil. The BEST. You will need to turn the fried egg over in the pan so that the yolk is quite well cooked, as yolk dribbling down your chin while in the car or outside is not ideal. Add the bacon, and some brown sauce, I suppose, or mustard. I find ketchup and egg a weird combination that does not work at all.

Full English

There are so many ingredients that go into making up the full English breakfast and I generally think there are far too many things on the plate, a bit like roast Sunday

One of the best things ever for a picnic breakfast is a bacon and egg bap.

lunch. For the person who is not a major cook, an English breakfast can be daunting first thing in the morning, even though you may have all the best intentions of wanting to impress your guests or family with such a treat. Here are a few tips.

Baked tomatoes, baked mushrooms, bacon and sausages can all be got ready and put in the oven until it is time to serve them, but I would wait to cook the eggs until the lucky people are there, as eggs generally have to go straight from pan to plate to mouth to be any good at all. If it all seems too much, you could do a Part English. A dish of glistening sausages straight from the oven with a pot of mustard and toast is perfect. The easiest way to cook sausages is to prick them about three times each on both sides, put them in a baking dish and pop into a hot oven for about 20 minutes. To check that they are cooked, cut one in half and if it is a bit pink put them back in for a few minutes. They should be browned a bit on the outside, too. Mushrooms or tomatoes on toast for breakfast is lovely and means that you don't shoot your bolt in one go. If you come up with everything the first morning, what on earth are you going to do for the next one? People are generally so grateful to come down and be offered breakfast that you should find any of these suggestions a success. And with the Part English, you use fewer pans so there is less washing up to get through after breakfast.

Foreign things

Think of doing half English, half French – for example, serving your fried egg with ham instead of bacon. You can also do this with prosciutto for a bit of Italian style – when fried, prosciutto becomes a most superior sort of bacon. I find that if I have had some prosciutto in the house for dinner there are often a couple of slices left over and breakfast is the perfect time to serve them. This works very well for Atkinsers, if there are any around.

Styling the English breakfast

I know that styling breakfast is something you're only going to do when you have time. But this is really easy and it can become as simple as laying the table. Tea towels make very good napkins: they are a great piece of 'ordinary' design that looks perfect at breakfast. Lay the table with tea towels as the napkins, a bottle of ketchup and brown sauce in the middle of the table with salt, pepper and sugar and you have a very stylish 'caff' look. It can be tempting to pack the table with jams, cereals and stuff, but sometimes you want to be a little simpler and you can add these things as you go along. I do think that the English tea towel is under used – it is also great as a tray cloth. I like to have a large supply of them; they are not expensive and it is nice to know there are plenty.

American breakfasts

Breakfast is one of the things that I love about being in America. The only problem is that it generally involves a lot of sugar and pretty awful coffee, so the joy of doing this at home is that you can have proper coffee with your pancakes. I love the combination of bacon and maple syrup, so find pancakes, bacon and maple syrup irresistible, as well as French toast with bacon and maple syrup. Making French toast is quite easy: soak pieces of bread in a bowl of beaten egg, then fry them on both sides until slightly brown. Use thick slices of bread and make sure that they really absorb the egg. Be as fancy as you like with the bread. Cholla or bloomer is good and this is also a good way to disguise stale bread – handy when you are far from the bread shop at 8 a.m.

For pancakes, buy pancake mix. American brands are best and if you can't find any in a shop locally, look on the Internet and find a site that sells American products. Pancakes can get quite elaborate. Add blueberries – or chocolate chips for very special occasions. American pancakes are much thicker than the sort we usually eat in Britain.

Bagels are good served toasted or, for a brunch-style meal, use them instead of toast with scrambled eggs and smoked salmon. Scrambled eggs should be quite runny to be good. This is obviously a question of personal taste, but for me there is nothing worse than scrambled eggs that are so cooked you can cut them with a knife. The thing is that once they start cooking in the pan they cook really fast. Never leave them, stir them all the time and when they look like they are just about ready lift them from the stove and put them straight on a plate. Each time you take the spoon around the pan the eggs cook more, so it is easy to overdo them at that point.

As children, my brother and I used to have scrambled eggs served on toast cut into small squares. Real bliss because you don't have to cut the toast. We were quite indulged!

For the American-style breakfast, use large red and white spot bandanas as napkins. I know that you are not going to want to have a whole load of different napkins for different sorts of breakfast, but the tea towels have many functions and so do these bandanas – they are marvellous on picnics and for lining baskets. I have shamelessly magpied this idea from my good friend Lucy, who is never far from one.

BIRTHDAYS

Coming down to breakfast on your birthday is very exciting, especially when there is a birthday chair waiting for you. Laying up for someone's birthday is great fun. Put a pile of presents by their place and provide a grand old chair at the head of the table. Breakfast on special occasions always deserves a bit of a fuss and so it is a good time to use special china and lay the table more glamorously than you usually would. Nothing too over the top, but treats are always a good thing. This is maybe the moment for the full English breakfast if that is the birthday person's favourite thing. Or bagels with scrambled eggs and smoked salmon. On my birthday pancakes would make me pretty happy. It doesn't really matter what the breakfast is as long as it is different from your everyday routine.

CHRISTMAS BREAKFAST

In our house, Christmas breakfast is always a bit of a roving affair. Somehow no one gets out of their dressing gowns until it is scarily close to the time when people start arriving for lunch, and by the time the stockings have been opened and we have eaten our chocolate oranges, breakfast seems to disappear slightly. Trays of coffee are really appreciated and some croissants, probably the last fresh ones we are going to see for a while because of the holidays, but then that is an urban Christmas morning. I have fantasies about what people do in the country, imagining a long breakfast table with a large family around it, all looking perfect in their pyjamas and dressing gowns.

If you do have to make Christmas breakfast, you might be a little nervous. It is one thing cooking a big lunch, but a big breakfast before it is a bit much. Get a large coffee pot and put that on the table and provide lots of croissants or delicious bread and good jam and let people help themselves. You could also boil up a load of eggs, now you know how easy it is (see page 61).

You will want the table to look pretty but you can't go crazy because you are going to have to turn it all around again in a few hours for lunch, so give yourself a break. Do something a bit mad like hanging mistletoe over the table, or put on a red tablecloth and save the rest for lunchtime.

If you want to have breakfast treats in bed with stockings, prepare the tray before you go to bed so that you can get the coffee going with ease in the morning. You can buy ready-cooked crispy bacon, but even if you have to cook it yourself it is easy – just bung it in the oven in a roasting tray. Add some sausages, which I love and are so easy to eat with your fingers. Frying all that stuff stinks the house out and you can't leave a frying pan, but cooking them in the oven is so easy and you can leave them to it – leaving the kitchen is always a good thing to be free to do on a busy Christmas morning.

You could also forget breakfast and do elevenses with something like cinnamon rolls from the last-chance bakery on Christmas Eve. I like the upside-downness of Christmas morning and I think that you should capitalise on this.

EASTER BREAKFAST

Easter breakfast is quite another story. As it is an egg celebration, breakfast can be one of the main attractions. You could go to town with a large centrepiece for the table or do a simpler, more tasteful option with armloads of spring flowers and a pretty cloth. I like both ideas, but let's start with going to town.

The Hallmark breakfast

This is especially good if you have children in the house. To be honest, if you haven't it's

a bit embarrassing, so go and find some if need be. When I talk about centrepieces, I mean those honeycomb paper things you get in card shops that open out into the shape of a huge Easter Bunny. You want high impact, with lots of pale yellow and mauve. You should be able to find paper Easter tablecloths in the same place as the bunny centrepiece.

My mother used to make us Easter baskets filled with eggs and a small present. She was quite indulgent – I do

realise that a lot of people don't want to give presents on all celebrations, but if you do it is quite fun to put in a silly t-shirt or something like that. I don't like the Mars Bar Easter eggs and others of their kind because they are ugly. Unfortunately, when going round the supermarket with my godson last Easter it was the Action Man Easter egg that attracted most attention, and the old-fashioned style papier-mâché ones filled with little eggs were not such winners. There has to be room for everything, so go with Mars, Action Man and the rest, but have the pretty stuff too. The good thing about Easter baskets is that they then double as baskets for the Easter egg hunt, which is the most important part of the day (other than church, of course).

The more wholesome Easter breakfast

If you don't want to go down the Hallmark route, you can make an utterly pretty spring table. I like terracotta pots or vases of narcissi on the table. Last year, when I was staying with friends in France there were fields of wild narcissi, which were beautiful and smelt delicious, I have never seen them growing wild in England, but there are plenty of daffs here, which are divine and their scent epitomises Easter for me. You need bucketloads. Put a cloth on the table. I think that a cloth for breakfast is a good indication that it is a special day. Look out in antique markets and shops for pretty Easter cloths. They are quite easy to find and come in small sizes that are fine for a breakfast table. The ones I like are white soft cotton or linen with embroidered flowers. They look like they were stitched in the thirties – very cottagey.

This breakfast table calls for boiled eggs, doesn't it? And of course they have to be coloured. Well, this is near impossible to do unless you have white eggs and have you ever looked for white eggs in the supermarkets here? We just don't have them. Instead, use special eggs like duck eggs as an alternative, or try to get white leghorn egg – try farm shops or farmers' markets. Get some food colouring or an egg decoration kit and colour away. Serve pink boiled duck eggs for breakfast and no one can say you're boring! You'll need pretty egg cups, too. A friend of mine, who is an illustrator, goes to those shops where you paint your own china and makes beautiful ones, which she gives as Easter presents. If you are at all artistic then this is a lovely thing to do.

HUNTER
GATHERING

HUNTER GATHERING

Shopping is the key to getting away with not being a great cook. Shopping and accumulating is not just about food. It is about everything, including trays for serving food, old silver spoons, horn salad servers and interesting glasses. And if you accumulate stuff over time, from car boot sales, charity shops, antiques fairs, souvenir shops in airports, foreign markets and department stores as well as fancy interiors shops, shopping will be a lot more fun and your table will have a look that is all your own.

I spend a lot of my time in junk shops, flea markets and antiques fairs. There is nothing I like more than poking about in a whole load of junk on the lookout for some treasure. I find things I would never be able to afford if I bought them new in proper shops. Even on the high street, things are often more expensive, the quality is usually inferior and there are a gazillion other items exactly the same. In junk shops you stand a good chance of finding something unique and much more exciting. Once you get started, it's fun to search for the right things, and when you begin to see a look come together on your table you will be very pleased.

SHOPPING FOR YOUR HOME

Shopping for china and other things for the table is a lifetime's work and can take you all over the world. At least it is something that you can do wherever you are – it might be a little excessive to travel purely for the shopping. Little dishes and bowls are lovely things to bring back from a trip. When I was on holiday in Istanbul, the friend I was with bought the most beautiful old bowl with the star and crescent in the centre. It makes a perfect vegetable or salad bowl, but it is also the loveliest reminder of a good holiday. When you are away from home, venture off the beaten track for your shopping. I search out markets and junk shops – another nation's junk fascinates me and the ways in which other cultures serve things are always interesting.

SHOPPING FOR CHINA AND OTHER THINGS FOR THE TABLE IS A LIFETIME'S WORK AND CAN TAKE YOU ALL OVER THE WORLD.

Buying from scratch

Buying all your cutlery and plates for the first time is a pretty daunting undertaking. However cheap you find things when you are buying in sixes or eights and it can end up costing quite a lot. The first time I did this I bought really cheap things, like plastic-handled cutlery in bright colours, which was very pretty but also quite bendy! My plates were absolutely standard-issue white and I still have them. Since then I've gradually added to my collection until the other day I had a clear-out of start-up mugs and cutlery. The rules have changed a lot since our parents were filling their china cupboards, so don't think in terms of whole services. If you see some glass plates you like, buy them for cheese, puddings or

It is quite liberating when you realise that you don't have to have a full set of everything.

first courses. If you see dinner plates that you love but they are too expensive to buy eight, just get two. A couple of plates are useful for serving and when there are just two of you for supper.

I saw the most lovely coffee cups recently but they were very expensive. I bought two, because I now know that after dinner you rarely serve eight espressos. There are always a couple of people who want tea and a few takers for milk. The cups were still a bit steep, but it is quite liberating when you realise that you don't have to have a full set of everything.

Tablecloths

There aren't many tablecloths I really like and I think that it's best to stick to white, since they are the easiest to boil-wash. You have to be able to boil tablecloths and napkins, as they will get grease and red wine on them. Again, antique markets are a good hunting ground for old damask cloths – they're so expensive if you buy them new. I love using heavy French linen sheets on the table. They look great, they can be washed at the highest temperature, and because the fabric is so thick you can get away with not ironing them.

Red-and-white check cloths are lovely, as long as they are freshly laundered. I am afraid this is important with table linen: if you aren't going to have it looking crisp on the table you are better not to bother. The red-and-white check looks good with red bandanas as napkins. Paper napkins are horrid and don't bother buying napkins or cloths that have any polyester in them. Napkins that aren't pure cotton or linen are not

nice to use and you can't wash them at such high temperatures so they will get stained eventually.

Large napkins are the best but hard to come by, so if you see any really big ones in antique markets, get them. New napkins are usually small, which is just cost cutting on the part of the manufacturer and annoying. I like having stacks of napkins and buy them in all colours for everyday use – a bore from an ironing point of view but they are quite easy things to iron. For children, I like big old hand towels to tie around their necks. You can buy these very cheaply, again in junk shops, and they are perfect as bibs, great for drying glass and good for telly suppers as they cover your lap with enough extra for your hands.

Melamine platters

These come in good colours and are quite easy to find. They are perfect for serving hors d'oeuvres before dinner and because they look so good they make even quite ordinary things – or at least easy-to-find things, like silver-skin cocktail onions, little gherkins, quails' eggs, little hunks of Parmesan or Pecorino – look great. This is a very easy way of doing a first course. Not only does most of it come out of a jar, but it also doesn't constrict you to sitting at the table, which I find impossible to do when I am trying to make sure the main course isn't overcooked.

China platters

Again, worth looking for in antiques shops or craft fairs. There is nothing nicer than putting a big serving dish with everything on it on the table. Whether it's bangers and mash, fish fingers with mash and peas, or a roast with all the vegetables, food looks really inviting on one plate. When you are buying china, bear in mind how things are going to work together. They don't have

LITTLE GLASSES ARE SO PRETTY AND CAN LOOK JEWEL-LIKE ON THE TABLE.

to match but the styles and colours should look good together and mix well.

You do, of course, have to think about the food too. You can't have a beautiful plate and serve filthy food, but if you keep to simple things you shouldn't go too far wrong. Even the simplest dishes look so much more appealing served on beautiful platters and people will think you know what you're doing. And very soon you will.

Glasses

I like buying different sorts of glasses. I often serve wine in small tumblers, something many people do in France. You can sometimes find these little green glasses that are wonderful and very cheap. You can use them for white wine, champagne or espresso, or for portion-controlled glasses of fizzy drinks for visiting children. Little glasses are so pretty and coloured ones can look jewel-like on the table. I don't think coloured glass is great for coloured drinks – blue glass makes all red drinks look like poison. But I do think you can serve white wine in green glass or in any pink or red glass, which also works for pink drinks.

Carafes

I buy old carafes for serving water rather than wine, particularly useful if you use a water filter instead of bottled water and so much smarter that a jug. If you have trouble finding old carafes, look out for the fancy bottles of lemonade sold in some delis and bottle shops.

They have china and rubber seal tops and make perfect water bottles.

Pint glasses

Old pub glasses have all sorts of uses. They are great for serving a pint of prawns in, which makes a perfect pre-dinner snack with some good mayonnaise. They're also good for serving breadsticks or long sticks of carrot with a dip, and for long chocolate bars after dinner.

FOOD SHOPPING TIPS

If you find a wonderful new deli, keep it to yourself for a while. Then you can get a few dinners out of it before you tell your friends. Food markets are good. If there is a farmers' market near you, use it, and you can usually put together a whole meal without having to cook anything. Buy things like dressed crab and potted shrimps for delicious weekend lunches or suppers. Keep an eye out for shops offering good things they make themselves. I found a new butcher the other day who is making his own delicious scotch eggs, pork pies and sausage rolls. The best butchers also have great sausages and if you buy good ones you can't really go wrong for picnics, breakfasts or bangers and mash suppers. You'll need different types for each event, and some good mustard – a sausage feast is all in the shopping.

If you live near a specialist shop, like a good cheese shop, take advantage of their knowledge and always ask their advice. Anyone who opens a specialist shop is going to be something of swot about their chosen subject, so they will love nothing more than chatting about it. With cheese, if you buy the right things you have a course without batting an eyelid. Serve a lovely piece of cheese on a pretty plate with a bowl of delicious salad and you're set.

Be adaptable

Wherever you are, tune in to what's around and adapt, rather than worrying about what you can't get. I find that when I'm in Scotland I eat and entertain in a very different way from when I am in London. There aren't lots of smart delis with wonderful food to take away, but there is the most amazing butcher's shop owned by a man called Mr Mustard. His beef melts on your tongue and can be cut with the side of your fork.

If you buy good produce it is very hard to foul it up and unless you overcook a good piece of beef it is going to be delicious. (If you're not near a good butcher you can buy wonderful meat mail order direct from the source.) In the summer there are the most amazing fruit farms selling Scottish strawberries and raspberries, and served with caster sugar and crème fraîche they take some beating as a pudding. And instead of putting the berries in any old bowl and plonking the tub of cream on the table, use some culinary trickery. Cream is much improved if it is put in a big old rummer glass, with a silver spoon. Both can be bought in antique shops or markets for not much money and look so pretty. For the berries, an old creamware pudding bowl looks lovely or a shallow glass dish. You can also serve the berries already in glasses with a dollop of crème fraîche on top.

Food to put straight on a plate

If you live in a city you will, without a doubt, have a deli counter near you. A good summer lunch or dinner is some cold beef (quite rare) from the deli, served with a good horseradish and a couple of salads. A regular green salad is easy enough to make and so is a mozzarella salad (see page 145); provided you can get your hands on some good mozzarella it really just needs arranging. If figs are in season they are also very good added to a mozzarella salad. I peel them because, although it might seem pathetic, I don't like eating the skins. Figs with prosciutto (Italian ham) are delicious and I think much better than melon, which is often served with prosciutto but which I don't really like at all. Up to you. Figs are a real treat and they go well in so many things – they're lovely slipped into a rocket salad with some balsamic vinegar. For a good rocket salad, though, you do have to trim the stalks, which can be long and unwieldy. It's worth this little bit of effort to make a much better salad.

Also at the deli or at your local Turkish or Lebanese takeaway you can find delicious dips like hummus and taramasalata, and little things like roasted peppers and stuffed vine leaves, which you can put on the table with some good olives and warm pitta bread for people to graze on. Just see what there is in the shop, keep an open mind and try new things. Always take the advice of the person serving – provided they know what they are talking about, they will lead you to try things that you wouldn't have otherwise. It is so easy to stick to the things you know and sometimes you don't even notice all the other yummy things that are on offer. Potted shrimps are another delicious first course and they are rarely served. All you have to be able to do is the toast.

Main courses without cooking

If you really can't bear to cook a main course, you could buy a rotisserie chicken. They are mostly very good, but roast chicken is so easy to make it yourself that it is better to do it if you can (see pages 142–5).

If you don't want supper to look like take-out night, get one thing and serve it as though you made it yourself. I was brought up on these sorts of dinners, like deli-bought cannelloni with salad. Most supermarkets will do a ready-made cannelloni or lasagne and, if you are careful, you should be able to decant it into one of your own dishes once you are home. Try to remember to buy a bottle of tomato passata, a carton of béchamel sauce and some extra Parmesan while you are there and they will be very handy for covering the top of the cannelloni or lasagne once you've transferred it. Better still is to get your local deli to make one for you in your own dish.

Some butchers will make steak and kidney, chicken or shepherd's pies for you, and it is always worth asking whether they will make them in your dishes. I do find pies a bit heavy to eat at night, though, unless it is really the dead of winter and you have had a very hearty day. The exception is shepherd's pie, which I am always delighted to see. Always have plenty of ketchup and Worcester sauce – never decanted, always in their bottles – on the table with shepherd's pie.

Take-out buffet

Buying a curry is the ultimate way to buy your way out of cooking and there is really nothing wrong with it at all. If you're keeping the origins of dinner secret (see the section on feeding your in-laws on pages 45–6) you need to get rid of all the foil boxes before they arrive. But if you're quite relaxed about people knowing where dinner's from you don't need to worry. Also, if you are serving a lot of people you can get more foil boxes in the oven than large dishes. So what you want to do is make sure that all your surfaces are clear and you have some large dishes waiting to receive the food. Empty your bin so it's ready for all the empty packaging.

If you don't want supper to look like take-out night, get one thing and serve it as though you made it yourself.

Lay the table like a buffet and put all the dishes in the middle. People can then perch round the table or help themselves and sit elsewhere. This does work and the point of having people to dinner is that they are gathered in a cosy and relaxed environment. As long as the food is good it doesn't matter who made it. I like hanging out, and if you are with people who like doing that too, this relaxed, buffet-style meal is perfect. No one gets stuck with anyone and you can move about easily and talk to more people than if you were seated at the table for the whole meal. This doesn't suit everyone though, so you need to be careful that you invite the right sort of people; some are better in a more formal setting. This approach also allows you to move freely in and out of the kitchen so when you run out of bowls and need to wash some up before pudding, you can do so without any stress. If you are easy about it you will probably find that either no one else notices or they are holding a tea towel ready for you to pass them the wet bowls.

Purchasing your way out of cooking is so relaxing and fun, because it is a question of choosing rather than sweating and I am not sure that the cost is really that different. When I go to the supermarket and buy dinner it always costs a lot. Takeaway is probably the same price or not that much more.

ARRIVING HOME WITH BAGS OF SHOPPING FROM THE OFFICE

At this point, I usually want to collapse into a bath instead of getting my house tidy and ready for the influx of guests. Sadly this is not usually an option, not immediately, anyway. The first thing to do is unpack the bags and take all the food out of its endless supply of plastic and polystyrene packaging. Throw away all the rubbish and take the bin out. This may sound a little strange, but if you are short of space it is important to get any excess rubbish out of the way, rather than unpack the ingredients as you cook. It helps keep chaos at bay. Then pour yourself a drink – whether alcoholic or not, it is calming – and put the radio or some music on. These small things make the preparations seem less like chores. Once you have got the first load of preparing done you can go and sink into a bath and relax for a while before people arrive.

PURCHASING YOUR WAY OUT OF COOKING IS SO RELAXING AND FUN, BECAUSE IT IS A QUESTION OF CHOOSING RATHER THAN SWEATING.

LAYING THE TABLE

LAYING THE TABLE

The way a dining table looks is important because it instantly creates an atmosphere. You can lay it the same way your whole life or you can have fun. I'm not talking about themed tables, so don't panic. But you can change the colour scheme with the flowers you choose, the type of glasses (coloured or clear), the napkins and tablecloth, and what sort of side plates you have. I must admit that I often don't have room for side plates because I'm always trying to squish too many people round the table. Your table won't always be immaculate; what matters is to have friends around it.

Sometimes I don't have a chance to do anything at all. Recently I spoke to some friends late in the afternoon and invited them over for supper that evening. I didn't get out of my last meeting until 7.30 and the table was still a desk when my friends sat down to pick at pitta bread and taramasalata while I was unpacking ready-roasted chickens from the supermarket and trying to sauté some leeks. Mercifully, everyone was pretty relaxed and the state of the table couldn't have mattered less.

FLOWERS

When you do have the time, take pride in laying a beautiful table and you'll make what could be a chore into a pleasure. Flowers look lovely, but you need to be careful about the height of the vases you use or they can form a barrier and make things feel very formal. Tall, slender trumpet vases or lily vases are excellent on round tables for big occasions, when you want people to be able to talk across the table to one another and not be hidden behind a huge bouquet. Lily vases are available in most high street homeware shops and they are not usually very expensive. You also often find them in antique shops – I saw about 12 the other day, all in pea-green glass. If you're having a big party and having lots of round tables, these vases give a room the height it needs. They can end up looking quite grand too, especially when they are arranged with foliage trailing down the sides.

At the other end of the scale there are few things prettier than flowers from your own garden. I had dinner with my friend Isabella one summer night and her house was filled with dahlias and sweet peas from her garden – so cheery and very seasonal. Dahlias are my new favourite flowers; they have a striking shape and colour and hold their own in a vase. Garden flowers can go into glasses, cylinders, old decanters, jugs, mugs, milk bottles – the more there are and the more unusual the container the better. Sweet peas are so pretty and smell so delicious I see no reason to use any other flower when they are in season. They look good in their country-cousin state of haphazard beauty or city chic at

YOUR TABLE WON'T ALWAYS BE IMMACULATE; WHAT MATTERS IS TO HAVE FRIENDS AROUND IT.

the centre of a table in square vases – or even one dumpy square vase – either mixed or in one colour.

My friend Plum told me about the loveliest thing that she saw at a dinner in New York recently – rows of gardenia heads down the middle of the table. Gardenias have the most delicious scent and their flowers are quite beautiful, although the bushes they come on are not.

You could do the same with tuberoses. As flowers they are not great-looking, but if you pull the heads from the stems, they do look pretty and the scent is heady. They smell stronger in the evening so are wonderful for a summer party.

I know that it is totally illegal to go into bluebell woods and pick flowers, so please be sensible with the following suggestion. Wild flowers on the table when you are eating outside in the country are lovely. They can be as simple as a bunch of bog myrtle and there is nothing wrong with picking a little of that. You will also find scabious and masses of nondescript little flowers on walks, and they can look lovely in an old teacup or a tiny glass on the kitchen table or terrace.

If you have clematis or climbing roses in your garden you'll find they look great arranged in a group of glass vases – I like the ones that are like short, dumpy cylinders. You will have trouble getting these sorts of flowers into normal taller vases as they don't have very long stems, so let them sit in the bottom of containers half-filled with water. You don't need very many flowers and even if the colours are different and the sizes of the vases vary it still looks marvellous. Potted flowers, such as tulips, lily of the valley or African violets, are also lovely on a table. They don't take up much space and they are good either in the middle of a round table or in a row down a long one.

CANDLELIGHT ON THE TABLE

The main thing you need to remember is to keep the lighting low. Candles are lovely, but I would avoid having anything scented actually on the table. If you want to scent the room where you're eating that's fine, but steer clear of anything too heavy or sweet. Light, citrusy scents like grapefruit are good. Don't worry too much. After all, when you have an open-plan living room you are likely to have candles nearby anyway, and one often sits next to women who wear quite strong scent. It's only really a problem if the candles smell disgusting and they will make you feel ill whether you are eating or not.

Generally I find I don't have much space for candles on the table, but what I really love is having small jars, each containing a few flowers and a candle. This way you tend not to see the actual candle, just the flickering glow among the petals. Another pretty thing to do is to wind some jasmine down the table around the jars. Candlesticks are best in abundance and they are worth collecting. The more you have the better they will look because you will probably have a selection of heights, which can save a table from looking flat. I tend to use candlesticks more on grander occasions than everyday, although if you happen to have a pair of silver candlesticks they look splendid in permanent residence on the kitchen table.

LIGHTING THE ROOM

Overhead lighting is not great and I would always advise using lamps, unless you have some amazing chandelier. If you ever see any candle wall sconces on your travels, consider putting them on the walls round your dining table. They look so pretty and it isn't dangerous to have lit candles in them while you are in the room. You could get them wired up, but it is hell to change wires in the walls unless you're decorating from scratch. If you do have overhead lighting then make sure you have a dimmer switch. It's easy to have them added if you don't have one already. If you are a fan of fairy lights then they are very good draped along a mantlepiece. The main advice I have is to keep the lighting low. Other than that it doesn't really matter. No girl wants to sit in bright lights at night – golden light is best for the complexion and you get that with candles or lampshades that are lined in gold or champagne tones.

SERVING DISHES

If your cupboards are full of beautiful dishes to eat off you are going to be a lot more excited about laying the table. This may sound like the sort of thing that only the most experienced hostesses are going to manage, but once you get into the swing of looking out for good things for your table you will find it hard to stop. You don't need that much, but you do need to be able to see a few different uses for any one item so it is multi-functional. The dumpy cylindrical vases I mentioned above get used to hold all sorts of things, including cream, sugar, flowers, dips and carrots. Two of them have spouts (they are antique knife cleaners) and I have used them as gravy boats.

I find that the dishes I buy inspire both what I serve at dinner and how. While I am trailing round markets I often look at things and wonder what they would be good for. China and glass are especially cheap if they are oddments – single glasses and plates seem useless to most people – but they can be real treasures when it comes to serving. Imagine how lovely double cream would look in a beautiful old rummer wine glass with a vintage silver spoon bearing some long dead person's crest. And you can probably buy both for less than you'd pay for the most ordinary new glass. Put the rummer on the table with a beautiful bowl of fresh berries and there will be a dozen mouths watering around the table – no cooking skills required. This is culinary trickery: your guests will all have eaten strawberries and cream a zillion times before, but yours is much more exciting because it looks so lovely.

Salad is another example. It is not terribly hard and basically comes down to how you chop, but the skill is choosing the right serving dish. I love using old

washbasins and they are not generally that expensive, especially if their matching jug has been lost or broken. They are also quite robust which means that you can take them on picnics. Salad served in a large bowl immediately looks better than when it's spilling out of a small bowl. Weird but true. Salad is never going to look appealing if you know that as soon as you delve in with the salad servers most of it is going to go on the table. If it's served in a large bowl you don't get this fear (not a good emotion to have round the table) and it just looks more generous (a very good emotion to have round the table).

Recently, however, I have started to serve salads on big plates – old serving dishes that were used to serve roasts and are easy to find in markets. I used to think salad would fall off a platter but it looks great piled high and somehow it's easier to help yourself from a flat dish than a bowl. Obviously you have to dress it first – I scrub out the kitchen sink and do it there (see page 31). You have the perfect amount of space to get the dressing evenly distributed, the high sides of the sink prevent it from ending up on the floor and once it is done you can pile it as high as you like on the plate.

SERVING STYLES

Once your meal is cooked there are different schools of thought on how it should be served. I have always loved the American style of lining the table with dishes of meat and vegetables that are passed along by the guests. Asking everyone to pass food to one another is good because it allows people to sneak an extra potato or another scoop of sweetcorn without anyone else

Salad in a large bowl immediately looks better than when it's spilling out of a small bowl.

noticing – something you can never do when you have to wait to be asked whether you would like seconds from a sideboard and then have to get up and walk across the room, feeling like Miss Piggy. Passing things to each other also encourages your guests to chatter from the start and get involved.

Whether you are putting everything on a sideboard, leaving it in the kitchen or placing it directly on the table it is important that you have got a selection of good bowls and dishes to serve everything from. They don't have to be matching, and they don't have to be fine bone china; in fact, I prefer it if they aren't. These are all things that you can find easily on travels abroad, delving around antique shops or even in your local shops on the high street, but what is important is that you have good, large dishes for serving food. Everything looks a lot more appealing on a good plate.

Old kitchen mixing bowls are lovely for potatoes and mix very well with creamware, which is beautiful, although quite expensive. The old stuff is really worth searching out – you can get these marvellous shallow bowls with spouts that I suppose were used in old dairies. Also look out for old spongeware and even pieces of lustre ware – Wedgwood does wonderful lustre jugs that are designed by Jasper Conran. Don't be afraid to mix antiques with new; mixing is good and it is even better when the things sit well together. It is not as difficult as it might seem for this to happen, because you will find while you are shopping that your eye is unconsciously drawn to similar styles over and over again. Alternatively, colour is a good theme to choose and even if everything isn't exactly the same colour you can choose things whose palettes work together.

EATING OFF TRAYS

Trays are a manageable size so an easy way to start producing and shopping for meals. Thinking about preparing a table full of food for lots of people is daunting but getting a tray ready is little and simple and does all the right things for me. First, a meal on a tray is mostly about styling, and second, there is only space for one cooked thing, if that. From a shopping point of view the tray is very good as you can only fit enough for one person on it, so you can buy a beautiful teacup and saucer, when you would normally think that was totally impractical. A single cup and saucer can be made by one of the top makers and have a relatively cheap price tag because of its lonely status. It's quite easy to find old tea sets as they are very unfashionable at the moment, but really worth looking at. Don't worry if they are missing bits like a sugar bowl or milk jug. You can easily use glasses for the sugar or milk, and if the teapot is missing, keep on looking for a single one. An old silver one looks good, but otherwise mix-and-match china is really fine.

For a tea tray, a tea cosy is key. We used to have one when I was a child, but you never see them now. According to my friend John a cosy is crucial for a good cuppa. Watching him make tea made me realise why I normally think that it a wildly over-rated drink. You can't just bung a teabag in a mug; you need a teapot and a cosy, which makes a totally different cup of tea. A pot of tea on the table feels so much better than being handed a mug of something that has been slopped together in a few minutes. As with all things that taste good, a little ritual is involved in making good tea.

The perfect brew according to John

First boil the kettle and warm the pot. To do this pour a couple of inches of water into an empty tea pot, replace the lid and leave it until the lid is hot. Throw out the water.

Different people have different preferences as to tea, but John recommends two bags of Red Bush tea and half a pudding spoon of Assam or Darjeeling loose tea (it is the loose tea that makes tea refreshing). Blend different teas to find what suits you, but stick to these quantities for a medium/average-sized teapot.

ASSAM
100g

By now the water in the kettle is the right temperature to pour over the tea. Give it a stir, put on the tea cosy and leave the tea to brew for five minutes. With a tea cosy the tea stays hot for much longer, but never top up the pot with hot water; always start again.

Laying a tray for tea by the fire

The fun thing about shopping for your teapot and tea set is that you can have different styles for different things. My friend John uses an old metal teapot with a wooden handle with a seventies tea cosy and china mugs. I have a 19th-century tea set with hand-painted flower swags, and the tea cosy I bought recently is white linen with embroidered violets. Arguably the best teapots are the brown pottery glazed type you can buy in most china shops and certainly in all the major department stores. They can be used with plain mugs or any sort of cups and saucers, probably the heavier variety rather than anything too fine.

The brown teapot is perfect for a fireside tea tray. Add a toast rack and some hot buttered soda bread with raspberry jam and you have the perfect winter afternoon tea. Soda bread is the key to success with this. It tastes so much better than other bread, especially when it is toasted. This is the perfect sort of culinary trick – the mere fact that soda bread is slightly different to what is usually served will have people thinking that you know what you are doing in the kitchen. They need never know that this is where it ends. You can buy china toast racks, which look great with this sort of teapot or look for silver ones in junk shops which will work better with a finer tea set.

Putting together these things is part and parcel of the enjoyment you get from sitting down to the tea and toast. People really do feast with their eyes first and something like this takes only a little time to prepare. Then you can settle down and enjoy chat or contemplation with the tea.

P.S. Depending on how Martha you are feeling you could rustle up your own jam, and I really mean rustle. I have always thought that it took at least four days to make jam and that you had to have a huge kitchen, not to mention bosom, and pick your own fruit. Well, not true on any of those counts. You can buy frozen raspberries in the winter or fresh in the summer, put them in a pan with half the weight of sugar and simmer gently for about 30 to 40 minutes. Do not boil or the colour will go dingy. That is IT.

A late-night tray

I often fantasise about guests and guest bedrooms (that I don't have) with beautifully made beds and bedside tables with jars of biscuits. Guests often arrive late at night after a long journey and need feeding. What better than a tray by the fire with some sandwiches? This is partly inspired by an article I saw about the perfect cheese sandwich, made with Poilâne bread and cheese from the Auvergne region of France. This is quite particular and you may not be able to get this sort of bread or cheese from the Auvergne necessarily, but you can adopt the spirit of the idea, which is getting the best produce and doing a simple thing well. The better the cheese the less you have to do to make it appealing. Some delicious cheese with hot toast and a glass of red wine is a lovely thing to find waiting for you and it is purely down to good shopping. It isn't even very expensive to buy at the top end of the cheese market. If you can't get to a good cheese shop, try buying online. You will find some very good suppliers.

The other lovely treat for late night supper trays is soup or scrambled eggs. The thing about eating at this time of night is that it doesn't really matter how simple the food is. In fact the simpler the better, because it is sort of like a midnight feast and needs to be instant and easy to eat off your lap.

You can prepare the tray before your guest arrives. Think how lovely it would be to be brought a tray late at night. This should inspire you. I find whenever I am doing stuff like this I just have to think of how I would really like it to be done for me. Remember a large napkin. It is so easy to forget and when you are eating with your hands you do need one and when you are perching on a sofa you rather want a big one. The trusty tea towel is good, not the grubby rag that has been hanging on the oven door for a week but a crisply laundered linen one with 'glasses' written down the side. Old linen hand towels are also good for these occasions. I love tea towels. I love having a

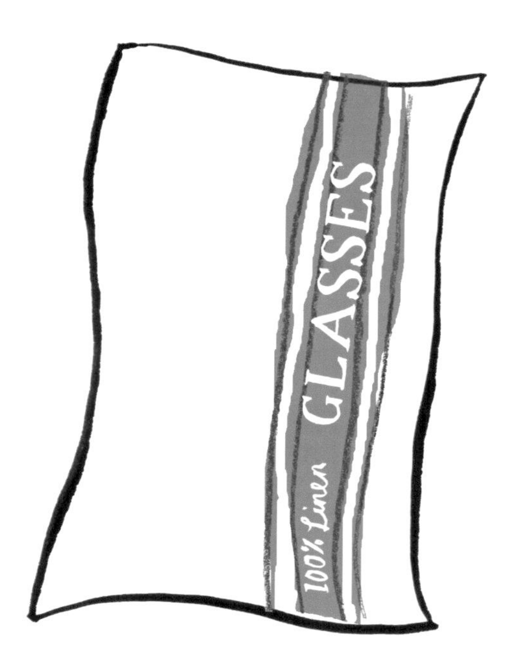

constantly high pile of them in the cupboard and I really like them to be pressed. I know it is a bit ridiculous and while I am ironing them I do wonder what the point is, but they are just so much nicer when they are pressed. The mother of one of my friends had loads of old-fashioned linen union tea towels with her initial embroidered in the corner of them all. They look so great and I am very envious of this collection. You have to keep nice tea towels strictly for drying glasses as you don't want horrid burn stains on them.

Tray cloths

At flea markets and antique fairs there is often someone selling 'heirloom linens' and you will almost certainly find tray cloths. No one uses them any more so you will get them for a song. A cloth will really complete the look of your tray.

I OFTEN FANTASISE ABOUT GUESTS AND GUEST BEDROOMS THAT I DON'T HAVE WITH BEAUTIFULLY MADE BEDS AND BEDSIDE TABLES WITH JARS OF BISCUITS.

THE DINNER PARTY

THE DINNER PARTY

I am a big fan of dinner parties, mine or anybody else's. They're an excellent opportunity to meet new people and to do a little flirting, which is good for everyone. Dinner parties get a bit of a bad rap sometimes – I think people fear they might be snotty and formal – but there's no better way of getting people together in a relaxed environment than to invite them to sit around your table. Far better than going to a restaurant with friends which can be expensive and not that relaxing.

I think people have two main worries when they are contemplating having a dinner party. The first is that they can't cook. Well – your guests aren't coming for master chefery. When was the last time you accepted an invitation to someone's house for dinner and thought about what you would be getting to eat? The second thing I've found people get anxious about is their home. Again, don't worry. You are far more likely to offend someone by not inviting them than by the size of your sitting room. Never feel insecure about your home and worry that it isn't good enough. I don't think you should ever be nervous of inviting anyone. If your reasons for asking them are right, they will be thrilled to be there, and you never know what friendships or connections will be made around your table. A dinner party is the easiest way to meet new people, and that really is one of life's fun things.

THERE'S NO BETTER WAY OF GETTING PEOPLE TOGETHER IN A RELAXED ENVIRONMENT THAN TO INVITE THEM TO SIT AROUND YOUR TABLE.

INVITING PEOPLE

I get a weird form of Tourette's syndrome when it comes to inviting people to dinner; I just can't stop myself, and so far it has never led to total disaster; slight chaos, perhaps. The thing is that however much I think that sticking to six is a good idea, if there is a lull in the conversation with a friend in the week before a dinner an invitation just sort of slips out, or I bump into someone that would be great to have there, and it just seems so pedestrian not to ask them because of the size of one's table – and before I know it I end up with many more people than I intended. In fact, it is worse than intended: it is more like more than I can fit. The thing is that it is always fine.

Last week I had a dinner where there were eleven people and my table fits six. I had got a little out of control and figured that it was just ridiculous to be governed by a piece of furniture and that it was much more important to have all the people you like around the table rather than only half of them sitting comfortably. Well, what I hadn't considered was that I didn't have enough chairs to sit on! In the end there were a couple of slipper chairs, which, although quite wide and very low, were fine, and one person was perched on a stepladder. It was in fact a great dinner, mostly because of the people that were sitting higgledy-piggledy around the table. The time that this is really not any good is when you have got stiff and slightly tricky people. One stiff or tricky person will be improved by this sort of situation as they will just have to get on with it, but you don't ever want more than one anyway!

The other thing that I find about inviting people is that the times that I have planned the guest list very carefully are never as much fun as the times when I have let it evolve. There was a time when, for some extraordinary reason, I gave three dinners in three weeks and the cast for all of them came together with a little help from me and a little from chance. There is always a protagonist, the person you bump into and invite because you haven't seen them for a while. Then wait and see who crosses your path. You might get an email from someone that you haven't seen for a while. This is what happened to me: my old friend Charlie and his wife had rather slipped out of my life and when I got a random email from Charlie I asked if he and Sof would come to dinner that night. Then Rowan called asking me to dinner, so I asked him to come to me instead. Finally there was a friend of mine I sent a message to saying that I was cooking dinner if he fancied joining and he did. This was one of the rare times I have been able to stick to six, and it was lovely; there were enough people who knew each other and a couple who didn't. With old friends you get an easy banter that keeps things flowing. If you have too many new people then you run the risk of those awkward silences.

I would always recommend that you ask like this as it really works. As with all things in life, if you leave a little to fate it all comes right. You can't over-arrange people – they are too fallible and mercurial but expecting a little less from them and a little help from chance is a method that I have found really come up trumps.

POINTS ON INVITING

1 Don't be too rigid when inviting. You have to be flexible. It is impossible to write a list of people and to expect them all to be available. Be freer than that.

2 Never plan a dinner too far ahead. People cannot possibly know what they are doing. I feel a bit trapped by people if I am asked to dinner months in advance. I am immediately suspicious and know for sure that nearer the time a dazzling invitation is going to arrive for something the very same night.

3 Always try to leave a gap in your guest list for someone you bump into nearer the time of the dinner. This is bound to happen and they will be the person that adds the sparkle.

4 Make sure that you have a combination of couples and single people. A dinner with couples only is never as much fun as a mixture.

5 Always be delighted when people say that their husband or wife is away. One half of a couple is always fun – for some reason they always behave differently when they are alone.

6 I was appalled the other day when a woman told me that she was never asked out when her husband was away (and he is away most of the time). Apparently hostesses don't like women on their own as they fear for their own husbands. If you have ever done this be very ashamed of yourself. Take another look at your mothy

husband and get real about how much the rest of womankind is desiring him. And have a little think about a time in the future when you might be a single woman again. Nothing is guaranteed forever.

7 If you want people to dress up tell them, and if it is your birthday let people know. There is nothing more embarrassing for people to arrive at your birthday dinner having no idea. I love my friend Katie who always starts talking about her birthday a good month before, giving you plenty of time to find her the perfect gift and keep the date clear, whereas Luella always lands it like a bomb on your lap the day before! (I love Luella too!) My godmother keeps it a deathly secret and won't let you know even while the cake is being brought out, and I love her too, very much!

AS WITH ALL THINGS IN LIFE, IF YOU LEAVE A LITTLE TO FATE IT ALL COMES RIGHT.

LAST-MINUTE EXTRA GUESTS

Try not to despair when you are asked if a guest can bring someone. If you don't have space or know that you loathe the person they want to bring then for goodness' sake say no – there is no point having your evening ruined because you feel that to be a chilled-out person you have to say yes. It isn't true and I have said no on occasions. Don't be bullied by your friends; they can be a bit bullying sometimes, even if they don't mean to.

However, more often than not it is worth saying yes. You never know who is going to be brought across your threshold and it always makes an evening more interesting. Even if they turn out to be ghastly, boring or rude they will have added some colour for the post mortem. I have met both greats and duds (whose names I can't even remember) this way but the duds were a small price to pay for the goodies. The duds don't matter but the greats would be a tragedy to miss. It is also important to remember that what goes around comes around and one day you might be staying with friends where you potentially are the extra guest at a stranger's dinner party. A policy of open door/space at the table is very important.

However, if you are going to ask if you can bring someone you always have to be prepared for the answer to be no without putting on a strop. Don't be offended or think that your hostess is uptight as a result; there is no point asking a question if you are not prepared for the answer to be no. There are also some people who seem unable to move without an entourage; this is very boring and a habit to be snapped out of.

PANICKING ABOUT WHAT TO WEAR

This is really common and it is one of those simple questions that rarely gets a helpful answer out of your hostess, should you ask. Of course this is only ever an issue when you are going somewhere you haven't been before, which always makes it doubly hard. I was asked to dinner in the country the other day and the dress was informal. This is a bit of a minefield, because that doesn't necessarily mean jeans; it can just mean that it isn't black tie. Don't worry too much about London clothes versus country clothes: black chiffon is fine if that is what you have got. As long as you look pretty then you can't really go wrong.

For dinner party dress I think that you have to be comfortable with what you are wearing, and when you have a room full of guests the chances are that the dress will be pretty varied. There are bound to be a few pairs of jeans, just because there always are, a smattering of little black dresses and some other varieties of dress. It doesn't matter as long as you are happy in what you are wearing. In my own house I always find it funny (that's funny a bit weird, not funny ha-ha) to dress up. Firstly I am usually barefoot, so even if I am in a dress it feels quite relaxed. You have to know what you like in your house and be clear about it. If you want people to dress up then tell them. There is no point being ambiguous about it. Everyone loves dressing up: it is great to sling on some heels and a dress. The dress code at my house is 'showered and changed', because however relaxed I am, I do think a bath and a clean shirt on a man is pretty much essential.

SHOPPING FOR DINNER

I like having dinners early in the week – a new thing for me; it's because you can get a lot done at the weekend. Find out if you have a farmers' market near you. These are the nicest places to shop and a lovely thing to do on a Sunday morning. I usually go with my friend Sarah. We shop very differently: she has three teenage children and so talks about things like running a fridge, which is something I have never considered.

You can get everything here, from the flowers to the meat, vegetables and cheese. The great thing is that you buy in season and can arrive not really knowing what you are going to have. It is perfect for a little culinary trickery. The last time I was there I got the most beautiful long basket of apples and pears from one stall. I put it on the table with cheese and salad and it got a lot of oohs and aahs. Apples or pears are a lovely thing to have with cheese and are often not thought of. The more alternatives to bread or crackers you can think of the better, as there is nearly always a low carbs person at the table.

The thing to avoid at farmers' markets is getting carried away with the choice of vegetables (this is more likely to happen in the summer than the winter). Remember that cooking vegetables is time-consuming and takes up a lot of pans. Don't get overexcited – you have to keep it simple, otherwise you end up spending a fortune, running out of space in your kitchen and getting in a terrible muddle.

I like shopping in small independent shops rather than supermarkets. I realise that this is a luxury I can afford because I am not bound by a 9–5 job or by having to run a fridge. I do use supermarkets sometimes: I particularly like shopping online, and if you remember the day before it's really brilliant as you can shop from your desk. It also means that you can go for prettier glass bottles of water rather than lighter plastic ones as you won't have to lug them home.

If you have managed to do your shopping on a Sunday then the final details can be left for the afternoon or lunch break on the day of your dinner. This is when you need to go and get the final treats. I will almost definitely go to my favourite cheese shop for some cheese or good oatcakes, my favourite greengrocer for a bag of cherries, or Baker and Spice for some of their amazing Florentines. With the main shop done you will have the time to flit about for the frivolities.

Try to leave work early. Strike a deal with someone you work with so that you don't take a lunch hour and leave an hour early. This will really help as you will have the time to get those last-minute things. I do find, though, that the more time I have, the more time I fill, so this isn't strictly necessary.

When you are short of time it is important to focus. Go to one shop – this is when supermarkets are sent from god. Write a list on your way there and don't try anything fancy and new. Get a couple of chickens, salad and new potatoes (depending on the season you can either roast or boil them).

If you can think of it in time then call your local wine shop – they will probably deliver. Lugging bottles of wine home is hell.

GETTING ORGANISED – KEY POINTS

There are things to watch out for – dinners can become formal and a bit stiff if you let them. If you're relaxed and confident that all is well, it will be. There are two important things to bear in mind. First, strike a balance between old friends and new; you don't want to end up with a room full of strangers. Second, don't try to cook something for the first time from a cookery book written by a three-star chef. It will be a nightmare. If you avoid these things your party should be fine. Take glitches in your stride. If you don't care about them, no one else will and they probably won't even notice anything has gone wrong.

Whether your dinner is smart or not is entirely up to you, and there isn't a right or a wrong way. Whichever route you decide to take, the principles for getting it right remain the same. If you are not in a position to appoint a team of staff to make the evening pass without too much stress on your part, my advice is this: keep it as simple as possible and do as much beforehand as you can. If this is an evening that cannot be informal and slightly haphazard, take the afternoon off work or even the whole day, so it will be a pleasure. Once you have time, you can do almost anything, but watch out: time is like space and if you have it you will fill it. I once spent a whole day preparing dinner and it was no better than the ones that I throw together at the last minute, and there was far too much food.

A dinner party shouldn't feel like a trial. Don't feel that you have to serve 'restaurant' food, which is what a lot of cookery books offer. There is something that restaurants can't provide and that is good home cooking – this is where you are ahead of the great chefs. In your home, you can provide comfort and atmosphere that can never be achieved in a restaurant. As a child, it always bothered me that you could never have seconds in a restaurant. I also didn't like their fancy puddings and the fact that they never offered chocolate or sweets at the end of lunch. Most restaurants still don't provide these services, but you can and should.

There is something that restaurants can't provide and that is good home cooking – or seconds.

If you have a husband or boyfriend, you are already ahead as you have a live-in barman – whether or not he knows it yet. I think that bartender skills run in male genes, so don't worry. Delegate all wine and cocktail responsibilities to him, as well as the music. These things are usually well within a man's remit.

APERITIFS

I have recently started offering aperitifs when guests arrive. I know it seems easier just to offer wine, but it's so much jazzier to serve a proper drink. My current favourite is champagne on the rocks. People accept this very gratefully and there is something about a tumbler of champagne that is indulgent and shows some largesse, which bodes well for the evening. Now, before you reel back in horror at the idea of offering champagne like beer, let me say it's not that terrifying. For one thing, if you're serving champagne on the rocks you can get away with something less expensive. The leading supermarkets usually have very good wine buyers and sell excellent house champagnes that are perfect for serving like this – and the price tag will not be that bad. Also, while a tumbler filled with champagne looks like you are giving a lot more than you would in a flute, you aren't because the ice takes up a fair amount of space and you end up with about the same quantity. Champagne looks great this way: the ice enhances the colour and a tumbler shows you mean business – it's the cocktail equivalent to wearing Chanel with ripped jeans. If you want to find a middle ground, use large, stemmed water glasses.

Bellinis and friends

Bellinis (champagne and peach nectar) and Rossinis (champagne and strawberry nectar) are good drinks to serve, particularly in the summer. Look out for fruit nectars in specialist shops and even in the supermarkets. Almost anything mixed with champagne and served in a large glass with ice is lovely – just be careful not to add too much fruit juice. Kirs and kir royales are delicious, too. Pour a *little* crème de cassis into a glass and add wine for a kir, or champagne for a kir royale.

More cocktails to try

If you do feel like coping with cocktails, here is my dad's list of his favourites; some are more complicated than others. Frankly, the idea of doing anything with egg whites before a dinner party sounds like far too much fuss for me, but you may feel differently. The great thing about serving cocktails is that you don't have to give your guests a choice. I think it's much nicer to be given a drink than be asked what you want. The fewer decisions the better, to my mind.

NEGRONI

- $^{1}/_{2}$ gin
- $^{1}/_{2}$ Campari

Serve in a tumbler on ice with a twist or slice of lemon or orange

AMERICANO

- $^{1}/_{3}$ gin
- $^{1}/_{3}$ Campari
- $^{1}/_{3}$ red vermouth

Stir well with plenty of ice and serve in cocktail glasses. Or mix and serve in tumblers with ice and a slice of orange. You can add a few dashes of angostura bitters.

BLOODY BULL

- juice of 1 lemon
- $^{1}/_{3}$ vodka
- $^{1}/_{3}$ clamato juice (tomato and clam juice)
- $^{1}/_{3}$ beef consommé
- Worcester and Tabasco sauces

Put the ingredients in a cocktail shaker with sauces, salt and pepper to taste, and shake vigorously. Serve as a cocktail but without ice or celery.

WHITE LADY

- $^{1}/_{3}$ lemon juice
- $^{1}/_{3}$ gin
- $^{1}/_{3}$ Grand Marnier (or Cointreau)
- dash of egg white

Shake well, pour and garnish with a stemmed maraschino cherry.

SIDE CAR

- 1/3 lemon juice
- 1/3 cognac
- 1/3 Grand Marnier (or Cointreau)
- dash of egg white

Shake well, pour and garnish with a stemmed maraschino cherry.

MANHATTAN

The original Manhattan cocktail was created around 1890 by Supreme Court Judge Charles Henry Truax, when he was president of New York's Manhattan Club:

- 2/3 rye (blended American) or bourbon whiskey
- 1/3 Italian red vermouth
- dash of angostura bitters
- a stemmed maraschino cherry

Combine the whiskey, vermouth and bitters in a mixing glass or pitcher. Add two or three ice cubes and stir quickly until well chilled. Strain into stemmed cocktail glasses and add a stemmed maraschino cherry to each.

Campari

I am currently delighting in Campari and I'm on a one-woman crusade to bring this drink back to our drawing rooms. I'm never going to start getting it together with a cocktail shaker when there is a room full of guests – I'm simply not a frustrated barman – but mixers are very jolly indeed. Campari and orange juice is good –

squeeze the orange juice fresh, unless you can buy a good fresh orange juice, and use blood oranges when you can get them – but the one I really love is Campari and ginger ale. It's a refreshing end-of-the-day drink, a real perk-you-up, and you will be amazed by how people's faces light up when you offer it. Serve with a lot of ice in a long glass.

Gin and vodka tonics

Gin is powerful but has a delicious scented aroma. I have always been rather snooty about gin and tonic, thinking of it as brigadier-ish, but it is actually rather good. And of course vodka tonics are always lovely. You need good ice and lemon with both. These sorts of drinks are not only delicious but also practical, as it's not always convenient to open a bottle of wine when someone has just popped in for a quick drink.

Non-alcoholic drinks

If you are looking for something for the non-drinkers, all the fruit nectars are good with a slug of fizzy water or tonic. I find that tonic doesn't dilute the flavour as much as fizzy water. Orange juice with tonic and a squeeze of lime is quite delish; so is cranberry with a bit of soda in the top and lime. If you have an Italian delicatessen near you, see if they have those little bottles of sanbitter in conical bottles. The drink is bright red and rather delicious.

I HAVE ALWAYS BEEN RATHER SNOOTY ABOUT GIN AND TONIC, THINKING OF IT AS BRIGADIER-ISH, BUT IT IS ACTUALLY RATHER GOOD.

CANAPÉS AND PRE-DINNER TREATS

I wouldn't bother with a first course. If you are reading this book I'm assuming it's because you are not particularly at home in front of the Aga, so don't make yourself a slave to it. Unless you are an accomplished cook, timing everything is hard, and first courses are an added complication that I'm happy to remove from my evening. I also think that very few people want to sit at a table for three courses. It's better if the time spent sitting at the table is kept to a minimum so everyone can move around and talk to whoever they want.

But people are usually hungry when they arrive for dinner so it's good to have something to keep the wolf from the door until the main course is ready. The answer is to have delicious things to pick at. My very stylish friend Jacky fills her coffee table with crudités, dips, little spring rolls, sushi and so on – everything is tiny and very enticing. She does lots of different things so everyone can find something that they enjoy, whatever their dietary quirks and likes and dislikes. She is much more considerate than I am but she's right – you do need to make sure there is something for everyone. Vegetarians, for example, have a peculiar habit of keeping this information to themselves until they arrive, or they think you will remember from the last time they came. I simply can't retain that sort of information.

Fresh vegetables

In spring and summer when fresh peas in their pods are available, have a colander full of them on the table, as though fresh from the garden. Let people pick them from the pods and eat them before dinner – they taste best like that anyway. Radishes are good served with salt or butter. Wash them, leaving their stalks on, and stuff them into a tumbler. If you push the stalks down into the glass the pink radishes will stick out at the top looking so pretty and perky. Put a little bowl of Maldon salt beside them or some proper farmhouse butter from a farm shop or specialist deli. My father always adds little bowls of gherkins, silver-skin pickled onions, thick slices of salami and pieces of parmesan. A

large tray with lots of small dishes like this and a stack of napkins beside it looks very chic.

Another idea is to have some bowls of cut raw vegetables – you can buy them already prepared or do them yourself, but I know what I would do. Then put out a little bowl of hummus or moutabal (an aubergine dip also called baba ghannouj) and some toasted pitta cut into strips. Always delicious and requires no culinary talent – the dips can come from the supermarket or a Middle Eastern restaurant or deli. Lebanese restaurants do wonderful bowls of crudités served on ice, which makes them look very enticing. If you have a Lebanese restaurant near you, it is definitely worth investigating their menu of first courses. Stealing ideas from any country that has a culture of either eating with their hands or having lots of small dishes is always a good idea.

Tapas

Spanish tapas, lots of little plates of meats and cheeses, are perfect for guests who are trying to do the Atkins diet. I love Spanish peppers called pimientos de Padrón, which are green and look like large chillis. They are delicious and eating them is like playing Russian Roulette because about one in ten is very hot. You simply fry them in olive oil and serve with some sea salt sprinkled over them. These are the perfect sort of culinary trickery – extremely easy to cook but hard to find so if you do manage to track them down you will wow everyone with your cleverness.

White bean dip

I got this dip from Donna Hay's book *Flavours*, but I've slightly increased the quantities. It tastes good and is easy to make if you have a food processor. Drain two cans of cannellini beans and put them in a food processor with a bunch of fresh mint, the cloves of two roasted heads of garlic (it is important when you roast garlic heads to scalp them, otherwise it is impossible to get the cloves out once they are cooked and hot), the juice of two lemons, four tablespoons of olive oil and some ground cumin and salt and pepper. Just keep tasting it and add more or less lemon, mint and seasoning as you like. You can also use basil or flat-leaf parsley or mix the herbs – whatever tastes good to you.

Don't let it get too dry – keep adding olive oil if it needs it. When the dip is ready, decant it into a shallow bowl, make shallow pools in the surface with the back of a spoon and drizzle on some good olive oil; it will look very professional. Don't worry if it looks like a lot as it's just as delicious the next day.

Choose your bowl(s) carefully. I like small ceramic or glass bowls and I've just bought a pair of antique glass coolers, which are quite tubby and perfect for this sort of thing. I fill them with dip and put them on a tray with a little plate of toasted pitta. This dip can also be part of a bigger meal. I would happily serve it in the summer as part of a cold buffet with ham, salads and baked potatoes.

Crostini

Toast some ciabatta bread, or any sort of country loaf, under the grill, rub it with raw garlic and drizzle some olive oil over it. You can buy many different toppings to pile on top of your crostini, including olive tapenade, aubergine or mushroom dips, and patés. A selection can look great together on a large dish. Look out for little jars of these sort of things in food shops in France. They are easy to find and store well. Italian delis also stock lots of pastes, including artichoke and walnut.

If you feel like getting handy with a knife and a chopping board, chopped tomatoes are easy to do. Peel the tomatoes (see page 36), cut them in half and scoop out the cores and watery bits. Chop the tomatoes up, season with salt, pepper, olive oil and basil and pile them on top of some toasted ciabatta into which you

One thing I think that you want to avoid is the lonely bowl of something in the middle of the coffee table.

have already rubbed garlic (see page 133). If you do this for people to eat before dinner, make the toasts bite-size. They are hard to eat otherwise and the tomato falls off – onto your carpet!

Artichoke hearts and other goodies

I love having little dishes of artichoke hearts and, if you can find them, sun-blushed tomatoes – sweeter and juicier than sundried. I do like sundried, too, and most supermarkets have them. Little chunks of Parmesan go well with all these goodies. Go to a good cheese shop or an Italian deli for the proper kind – Parmigiano Reggiano. It is produced under very strictly controlled guidelines by a small producer and is utterly delicious. This is the ultimate sort of culinary trickery: when you get the best you don't have to do anything to it and you feel clever for just finding it. All these things keep well so stock up when you have the chance.

Sushi

Sushi is a perfect thing to have pre-dinner, but there is no way you can make it yourself so you have to get takeaway. If you live in a city, sushi should be easy to find. Don't get too much – two types of sashimi and two types of roll is probably enough. Too many different things look a mess. Another idea is to serve some edamame, which you can buy in oriental supermarkets. These are fresh soya beans and they're yummy. Boil them for a few minutes, sprinkle with sea salt and just suck the beans out of the pods.

COCKTAIL NAPKINS

Now a lot of the things I've mentioned can be dripped or slopped, and I do get a bit twitchy when soya sauce or olive oil start heading towards the upholstery. I like to think of myself as totally chilled out, but there are some areas where I become really quite bourgeois and this is one of them. What you need is a pile of cocktail napkins, just like our grandmothers used to pass around. I think it's pretty to use old handkerchiefs – you see lots in markets for next to nothing because no one uses hankies any more. Otherwise, build up a collection of little white cocktail napkins. As well as wanting to protect carpets and upholstery, I often want a napkin to wipe my fingers.

How much of all the above you do depends on how many people you are having to dinner and what works for you. But one thing that I do think you do want to avoid is the lonely bowl of something in the middle of the coffee table. It's highly likely that no one will touch it, as people can get very self-conscious about making that long move from the sofa. I know this sounds silly, but you can feel a bit greedy if you're the only one. I have, but then I am quite greedy. Passing a plate of things can feel a bit awkward too. The best thing is to come into a room with a plate of something and hand it to someone else to pass around. If you have children, get them to do this.

DECIDING ON THE MAIN COURSE

Although I always mean to decide what I'm going to serve three days before the event and buy and cook ahead of time – and that's what I tell everyone else to do – the reality is that I often don't have time. That's why roast chicken has become my salvation: I simply can't think of anything else while I am standing slightly panicked in the supermarket. I know where I am with a chicken and more importantly I know which aisle the chicken is in. The more you cook something, the better you will become at doing it. There's nothing wrong in doing the same thing, provided you don't serve it all the time to the same people in close succession.

If you're really short of time, curry is always a good thing to serve at dinner parties because most people love it – see pages 45–6 and 87–8 for more on this. You can even slip in a vegetable curry for any undercover vegetarians. But as I said before, don't bother trying to make curry yourself. I have – once – and it was the most disgusting thing I have ever either produced or tasted. Virtually every city and town, even some villages, has a Thai or Indian restaurant, so there is no need to put yourself or your guests through this torture.

If you're preparing a simple dinner, keep it simple and don't try to serve too many things. For example, you may think vegetables are easy and want to serve lots of them, but it's hard to get them all cooked at the right time. They all have to have a different saucepan and if they are overcooked they are disgusting. To be a success, a simple dinner has to be really good. Here are my standbys for simple but delicious dinners.

Fillet of beef

Serve an excellent fillet of beef with a rocket salad and that is all you'll need. If your produce is the best available, you won't be able to afford anything else! But with good produce, you don't have to fuss around with periphery nonsense like sauce and 85 vegetables. It's such a shame to smother a fine cut of meat with a whole load of other stuff and it's difficult to get all of it on the table at the same time. It can also feel too heavy to eat late in the evening.

This type of simple fare must be presented very beautifully so people don't feel cheated. There is nothing lovelier than a heavily starched tablecloth and napkins, candles, a bottle of claret, and salt, pepper and mustard on the table, ready for the arrival of a fine, juicy fillet of beef sliced very thinly. If a tablecloth is going too far, do without and just have the napkins.

If you do want to serve a cooked vegetable, have asparagus when it is in season. And if you lose your nerve and feel that you must serve potatoes, chuck some small new potatoes, any kind, into a baking tray with some olive oil, rosemary and salt until they are cooked. They usually take about half an hour to 40 minutes and are delicious. This is the cheat's way to do roast potatoes: they don't have the fat of normal roast potatoes and you won't have to face the crispy crisis, because these aren't meant to go crispy anyway.

This is an excellent dinner and all you have to concentrate on is not overcooking the meat. A fillet never really takes longer than 20 minutes, then it should be left to stand for about 15 minutes. Before you put the meat in the oven you need to seal it. If you have an Aga you can just put it down on the hot hob for a flash on each side – it is quite exciting doing this as it makes a really loud sizzling noise. If you have a normal stove, heat up a pan without any fat and do the same. Sealing stops the juice from coming out while it is cooking so prevents the meat from drying out. *Any piece of beef should be sealed, so whatever cut you are roasting, seal it first.*

Twenty minutes in the hottest of ovens will produce a deliciously rare fillet, which is how I like it. If you have a good piece of beef it will melt in your mouth. If you like medium or even fairly well-done meat, leave it in for a little longer. If you aren't sure whether your meat is cooked, stick a skewer into it. If it comes out cold, the meat is still raw or very rare; if it's warm, the meat is medium-rare; if it's hot, the meat is well done. Otherwise, slice it open – this is what I usually end up doing. It's not very elegant, but it gives you a pretty clear answer.

Butterflied lamb

Lamb is easy to cook. Breaking my own rules again, I first made butterflied lamb when I had 14 people coming to dinner and no idea how I was going to fit them all in my flat, let alone how I was going to get anything on the table for them. At four o'clock that day I was still sitting in a café, having a cup of tea with a friend. Another friend, who was coming to dinner that night, walked past and asked what we were going to eat. I told him that I had no idea and fortunately, as he is a restaurateur, he did have some idea of what to do in the dinner department. Fate had really come up trumps. He told me to go to the butcher, get a leg of lamb and ask them to butterfly it. I didn't really understand what he was talking about but hoped that the butcher would. I went off to the shop and the first thing the butcher did was laugh at me when I asked for a leg of lamb to feed 14. That alarmed me slightly, until he said that lambs didn't come that big and he could give me two legs. Once over that hurdle, I nervously muttered the butterflying part, sure that he would laugh at me again and worse: ask me what I was talking about. Amazingly, he just went ahead and removed the bone. Some people argue that all meat should be cooked on the bone for the best flavour, and they are probably right, but this is too easy to get snooty about. Being boneless is what makes this lamb so easy to cook and carve. Roast lamb when it's on the bone seems a big deal for dinner, too much like Sunday lunch, but this is good served warm, at room temperature, in spring.

Once home, you marinade the meat. Pour some olive oil into a bowl with a few crushed cloves of garlic, rosemary, salt and pepper, put the meat in and leave it there, turning it a few times, for as long as you've got. If it's only an hour, that's better than nothing, but leave it longer if you can. Lay the meat out on a baking tray and stick it in a hot oven for about 40 minutes – it doesn't take nearly as long as a conventional leg with a bone. The timing of this really depends on the size of the leg and also how pink you like it. When the lamb is done, take it out of the oven and let it stand for about ten minutes – put some foil over it so that it doesn't get cold.

Slice it in long slithers, put them on a platter and pour over the meat juices from the pan – this is an Italian rather than an English way to serve lamb. All you need to serve with this is a rocket salad and maybe some of those roasted new potatoes I described on page 137.

You can use thyme instead of rosemary with lamb if you like. My friend Peter rolls his butterflied lamb with garlic, thyme, salt and pepper, roasts it for about 50 minutes and lets it sit for five minutes. Start cooking lamb and the more often you do it, the more confident you will become. You will get to know how long it takes in your oven and how you like to season it.

Roasted cherry tomatoes

If you want to do something else and have the time, Will's other suggestion that day was an excellent first course if you do want to have one – roasted cherry tomatoes. (You can serve everything together if you prefer.) Dump the tomatoes in a roasting tray with some balsamic vinegar, sugar and salt and blast them in the oven until they start to explode and caramelise. Toast some slices of sourdough bread under the grill, rub them with garlic and drizzle with some olive oil, and serve them with the tomatoes on top. I followed these instructions blindly, and they worked. The dinner was a huge success, and I was praised for my excellent cooking skills! Can you believe it?

I really like things to be multi-functional, whether it is a recipe or a glass. Once you can roast a tomato you have quite a lot of options open to you. As well as dumping them on the sourdough, you can turn

WITH GOOD PRODUCE YOU DON'T HAVE TO FUSS AROUND WITH PERIPHERY NONSENSE LIKE SAUCE AND 85 VEGETABLES.

them into a soup (see page 228), a pasta sauce or a salad. This is handy, because you can't keep that many different recipes in your head and referring to cookery books all the time is, frankly, tedious.

After all that lamb and tomatoes, you don't really need to offer anything other than coffee and tea with some treats. I have to say that I do like to have something sweet at the end of dinner, even if it is just a bar of chocolate.

More about lamb

All lamb is good. I love cutlets and chops as well as roast lamb. They all benefit from being left for as long as possible to marinade in some olive oil and rosemary as described above. This makes the meat lovely and tender when you cook it and gives it good flavour. Yesterday I had lunch with my friend Tanya, who had made lamb chops and salad – the most delicious and perfectly complete meal. We had a very mustardy dressing on the salad and it was yummy. Just mix olive oil with mustard and salt and pepper to make thick dressing. It lasts for a while, so don't worry about making too much. While lamb chops and a big green salad are quite rough and ready, even rustic, cutlets are more refined and proper. Both are delicious. I made dinner for my friend Lucy the other night; we had roasted cutlets with some potatoes and broccoli – so civilised and very French bistro.

CHICKEN

Roast chicken used to be my staple for dinners. In winter, there is nothing more inviting than walking into a house to be met by the delicious smell of roasting chicken. It is also exceptionally easy to cook and requires very little fuss. You can serve chicken all year round. I like to alter it slightly with the seasons, depending on what vegetables are available and the temperature outside.

If you serve roast chicken on a good serving dish you can get away with not really knowing how to carve. Cut the chicken up like the French do, removing the legs, thighs, wings and breast and laying them out on a plate. Cut the whole breast off the chicken and slice it. People can help themselves to the pieces that they want rather than having to announce their preference to the carver – just a little easier and more relaxed. Tongs make serving much easier too.

Winter chicken

Keep some butter out of the fridge so that it's soft, like a thick body cream. Rub the chicken with garlic and then with the butter, as if you are moisturising its skin, and sprinkle with salt. The butter and salt will make the skin crispy. I stick all sorts of things up the chicken's bottom, depending on what I have remembered to buy: onion, garlic and herbs. Rosemary is a good herb to use, or thyme or dill, tarragon, if you like its strong flavour – pretty much any of them work. Bung the bird in a hot oven and cook for an hour to an hour and half, depending on its size. If you aren't fussy about crispy skin, it is a good idea to cook your chicken upside down so the juices drip down into the breast and keep it moist. You can turn it the right way up towards the end of the cooking time to give the skin a chance to crisp.

The great thing about roasting chicken and new potatoes is they simply go in the oven until it is time for them to come out.

During the cold months I like roasted vegetables with chicken. Fill a baking tray with new potatoes covered with olive oil, salt and rosemary, and throw in some parsnips and carrots, too. My new favourite, shallots, can be put in whole with a roasting bird and some whole bulbs of garlic. Scalp the top of the garlic bulb first so you can get the garlic segments out when cooked. They look lovely – not to mention very professional.

The great thing about roasting chicken and new potatoes is that they simply go in the oven until it is time for them to come out and be eaten, no fuss. This leaves you time to do any amount of other things, like have a bath and get ready, tra la la. It also means that you can tidy up the kitchen, because it is so much easier to do anything if the surfaces are clear. I find that the place descends into chaos very quickly once all those baking trays start to come out of the oven. Another reason for keeping things simple.

Having said that, I do love bread sauce with chicken. It is one of my favourite things and I have always made it from a packet of bread sauce mix. Remember to get extra milk while you are out shopping, as you will need about one and half cartons. I like bread sauce quite thick, but that depends on your taste. This is also something that for some reason restaurants never ever serve, rather like they never seem to have any redcurrant jelly when they serve lamb – drives me crazy. Yet more easy ways to be ahead of the fancy chefs and people love these sorts of things.

Summer chicken

In summer, chicken can be served at room temperature and you don't need all those roasted vegetables. I like lemon and olive oil with summer chicken for a fresher taste. Put lemon halves, garlic and herbs inside the chicken, rub some olive oil over its back with your hands, and sprinkle with salt. The more you cook chicken the less you will have to think about what you're doing to it. It is simply a case of putting something on its back to encourage crisping and something inside it to give it juice and flavour. I am very happy to serve a summer chicken just with salad, end of story. Sometimes I might add new potatoes and some other spring vegetables of which there

I THINK THE KEY TO A GOOD GREEN SALAD IS TO ADD SOME HERBS. IT ALWAYS GETS A GOOD RESPONSE WHEN I DO THIS.

are plenty. I love to put fresh peas in the salad or you could even have a delicious mozzarella and tomato salad as another dish. All these things require little time and effort if you buy good produce.

SALADS TO SERVE WITH CHICKEN

A mozzarella, tomato and basil salad is a lovely summer dish. Buffalo (or bufala in Italian) is the best mozzarella, and while not essential, is probably worth the extra money if you can get it. Mozzarella comes in little bags of water to keep it moist so be sure to drain it properly or you get a watery salad. You can break up the mozzarella with your hands rather than slice it, and you can also rip the tomatoes, having taken out the pips, core and watery bits – this is a question of taste, of course, and there are people who like to keep those in. Buy a bunch of fresh basil and rip that liberally over the salad, then drizzle on some good olive oil and a little balsamic vinegar, depending on your taste.

Green salad

I think the key to a good green salad is to add some herbs, I don't know why more people don't do this, but I always get complimented on my salads when I do it. Mint is fabulous in salad and in the summer fresh peas are delicious in there too. Basil, dill and flat-leaf parsley are all good and coriander would work if you like it. I think coriander is perfectly horrible, and there are others like me, so I would be careful of using it too much. I often just drizzle my green salad with olive oil, lemon juice or balsamic, and some salt and pepper.

Endive salad

Endive is delicious and is also rather lovely to look at, particularly when mixed with purple radicchio. When you buy radicchio, go for the small ones and rip them, instead of chopping, so you keep the shape of the leaves. Endive salad benefits from a grainy mustard dressing, which is easy to make. Pour olive oil slowly into the mustard with salt and pepper and keep tasting until it's right. You don't need much vinegar as mustard can be quite vinegary already. Dress the salad at the last minute and add the dressing a bit at a time; there's nothing worse than a saturated salad. Mixing with your hands gives you more control than you have with salad servers.

Green bean salad

Green bean salad is the perfect thing in summer. Just be careful not to overcook the beans. When they're ready, run them under the cold tap to prevent them from cooking any more – this helps keep their fresh green colour too. Finely slice some red onion or shallots and add them to the beans – I like to chop the beans in half so you can eat everything with a fork. The mustard dressing for the endive salad works for this salad, too, or just add some good olive oil, a little lemon and maybe some fresh thyme, salt and pepper. For more salads, see pages 29–31, 34–7 and 44–5.

BANGERS AND MASH

I really love this. It may not be the thing to serve at your fanciest evening, but for cosier evenings it's perfect, because everyone loves sausages and mashed potato, and there are such good sausages available. It's nice to have a mixture of different sorts of sausages; your butcher should have a good selection, but so do supermarkets. Spike your sausages and put them in a baking dish in the oven – much easier than frying them, which smells, and you can leave them to cook by themselves. Make the mash (see page 150) and add a dollop of mustard or horseradish if you like. Then serve both the bangers and the mash on one big dish in the middle of the table. You can mash things other than potatoes, of course. Turnips are delicious mashed and so are swedes and celeriac, which are good alternatives for anyone trying to stay off potatoes.

The definitive word on mashed potatoes

The first thing about mashed potatoes is to boil them to death. The softer they are, the easier they are to mash. Drain well and return them to the pan. Use a good hand masher – beware of the blender, they will go gluey – and once you have roughly broken down the potatoes, add a generous knob of butter and mash again. There are many routes from here. My friend Peter uses lots of crème fraîche, which is lovely if you have it, but milk is absolutely fine. The main trick is to put the pan back on the stove before you add the crème fraîche or milk. Pull the potato to one side of the pan and pour the milk or cream into the empty part and heat. Once it's hot, combine it with the potatoes; this makes much better mash. A lot of people use olive oil instead of butter to be healthy. I say, if you're eating mashed potatoes stop kidding yourself and get on and enjoy them.

You can flavour your mash with all sorts of things:

- Mustard and/or horseradish. If you can find grated horseradish, this is a good time to use it.
- Cheese. Grated cheese mixed into your mash is delicious. It will melt and yummify.
- Garlic. Fry some chopped or crushed garlic in butter and mix it in at the last minute.
- Truffle oil on top of mashed potatoes is very good. Quite a grown-up taste so I would avoid doing this if there are children about, or just make two bowls. Very good with almost anything and an excellent accompaniment for roast chicken.
- If you have any flavoured oils, such as rosemary oil, blend some into the mash. Rosemary is very good with lamb.

COOKING FISH

Fish has a lot going for it. It is extremely easy to cook, tastes delicious and is good for you. Many vegetarians will eat it and so will dieters. The first time I cooked fish was through no choice of my own. (It takes me a long time to venture off into a new recipe, actually, just to venture off roast chicken.) I was presented with a piece of wild salmon by my then flatmate's mother to cook for her darling, ailing son. They are a family of great cooks. I come from a family of great shoppers. I had never cooked for him before, because he always cooked for me and I used to lay the table while he scattered flat-leaf parsley all over the kitchen floor as part of his culinary theatricals. But his mother had dropped off this wild salmon for him and it was up to me to turn it into our dinner – he was too ill even to give directions.

You can do quite a lot of cooking by common sense and thinking of things you have seen done before. Having eaten fish wrapped in parcels in restaurants, I decided to wrap the salmon in foil as I figured that it wouldn't dry out that way. First, I squeezed lemon juice over it and added olive oil and some salt I had bought in Paris because it came in a nice jar (my reason for buying anything, which thus far has served me well). The fish was a triumph in some ways. Rowan, my sick flatmate, was not too ill to tell me wryly that the Portuguese would probably have loved it – I had been far too enthusiastic with my fancy salt. But, apart from

this minor flaw, the fish was perfectly cooked and I knew that next time I just had to hold back on the salt. The salmon was still slightly underdone in the middle, which I like because it means it is juicy. Remember, the first time you make anything it is rarely great; you have to keep at it. Which is why it is not wise to open a cookery book and launch into some new and complicated dish when you have got eight people coming to dinner.

Since then I've always had great success with fish. Wrapping it in foil is the simplest and the best way as far as I am concerned. It can be adapted to almost any variety of fish and you can add all sorts of different flavourings. Things that are good to put with the fish are lemon, herbs – thyme or dill, fennel is very good if you slice it and lay the fish on it – ginger and spring onions, little shallots, cherry tomatoes. Olive oil is a must, and wine if you want. These are the things that will make it tasty, and if you pick two or three things from the list you can't go wrong.

Sea bass

If you're only having a few people to supper sea bass is wonderful, although quite expensive. The fishmonger will prepare it for you, so all you have to do is stuff its belly with dill or rosemary, add a little lemon or white wine, then wrap the fish loosely in foil before baking. Bake it for about 10 minutes if it's small, longer for a larger fish, and then check it – when you open the foil, steam should rise up. If it doesn't, the fish definitely needs to go back in the oven, as it isn't even hot yet. The best test is to see if the flesh comes away from the bone easily. There is nothing wrong with the centre flesh having that slightly translucent look – overcooked fish is a travesty, dry and very unappealing.

Trout and salmon

Trout is ideal cooked this way and so is a salmon tail, and if you can get wild salmon, so much the better. A whole salmon is perfect for feeding a lot of people and I think it's much tastier baked than poached.

Buying tip

My other advice is to buy the fish that has travelled the least distance, or at least if you are in an area where there is local fish, buy that. Recently I was in a supermarket in Scotland with my friend Glen, who wanted to get some sea bass. Beside the bass were some delicious sea trout. I insisted we got the trout; although sea bass is a fancier fish, the trout was local and the bass had come from Greece and was twice the price. Imagine how you would feel if you'd just arrived in the north of Scotland from so far away compared to an hour away by road – well, the same must apply to a fish.

A THING OR TWO ABOUT VEGETABLES

Starchy vegetables are very heavy so I prefer to serve green veg. French beans and Brussels sprouts are good and if you can get them ready prepared, so much the better. My very favourite is broccoli. When I'm ill, it's what I crave; when I have a hangover, it's all I want; and when I am well I love it too. There are two ways to cut broccoli: very small so that you have little florets, or with long stalks, which I also love because the stalks taste so good. Cook broccoli by boiling or steaming, but don't cook it for too long, as you want it still to have its crunch and great sharp colour. To serve, drain thoroughly and put it in a serving dish with olive oil, a squeeze of lemon, and some salt and pepper. This dressing makes a huge difference to broccoli and the same goes for broad beans, peas, spinach, asparagus and any of the water-based vegetables you can think of, such as courgettes.

A little courgette dish

Talking of courgettes, I find they are very easy to overcook, and overcooked courgettes are very disappointing. My friends Alan and Louise came to cook at my house recently. It was midwinter and their boiler had given up on them, so, desperate to be out of their igloo of a home, they came over and offered to make me dinner. Alan sliced courgettes into long thin strips and fried them in a pan in a little olive oil. He served them as an appetizer while we waited for the rest of dinner to be ready. Courgettes are delicious this way and I have made them quite a lot since. They should be slightly browned on each side but still have some of their crunch; if you have a griddle, cook them on that. You can only cook a few at a time so don't try to do this for lots of people, but for four, it is a delicious and quick to do.

Sautéeing

This is really a fancy word for frying but a good way to keep vegetables crunchy. Leeks are good cooked this way – chop them up and put them in the pan with some olive oil. They take a while, because actually this is the one thing you don't want to be crunchy, although you do want them to keep their colour. This method is also good for courgettes and okra, which I love and have always avoided buying, as I have never known what on earth to do with it. I still haven't worked out how to make okra like they do in Indian restaurants, but if you chop them and sauté them with a little olive oil (keep the pan quite dry), they are good and they don't go slimy which is a bonus.

I still haven't worked out how to make okra like they do in Indian restaurants, but if you chop them and sauté them with a little olive oil . . . they are good and they don't go slimy which is a bonus.

CHEESE COURSE

If you are serving a light main course, people will have room for salad and cheese. And if you're worried about not serving a proper first course, this gives you the extra course in a more relaxed way. This is the way they do things in France – they serve small courses but more of them. The great advantage of cheese is that it requires no cooking, just a little shopping. It can be a good back-up plan too: I have served the cheese course first in the past, when dinner was taking a bit longer than anticipated and there were some hungry faces around the table.

There is such a vast selection of cheeses that I get quite overwhelmed at a cheese counter. I never know what to choose and all too often end up with something quite dull, simply because I have chosen something that I know. Panic not – chat to the assistant behind the counter. Say what else you are eating and whether you want a hard or soft cheese. You can also try things, which helps enormously, so don't be afraid to do this. I always used to be embarrassed about tasting cheeses and felt that if I tried one I had to buy it.

I love serving just one cheese. It looks much more elegant and shows confidence in your choice, which is very important. If you look like you know what you're doing, the chances are people will believe that you do. And when you serve a single cheese you can just pass it round the table and people don't have to stop talking to help themselves – much easier than all the endless questions you get about what is what when you serve a plate of cheeses.

The perfect cheese to serve alone is a vacherin. It is the most delicious creamy cheese and it's seasonal, which makes it all the more desirable. The season is between October and the end of March. Serve it with a silver spoon and a green salad – the spooning of the vacherin is one of the things that I really love about it so make sure that you have a good spoon. This is one of the rare times that an odd silver pudding spoon is really useful.

Stilton is *the* winter cheese. Rich and strong, a drum of this will keep you going for some time. Again, it is something that I like to attack with a spoon, which accentuates Stilton's softness. Oatcakes are what you need here or celery. If you decide to have celery, put it on the table in a beautiful celery vase. Look out for these in markets and antique shops; they look like stemmed vases and keep the celery from drying out, and can also be used as flower vases.

Small truckles of Cheddar are great, when you don't have a major household to feed, and look rather adorable. Cheddar is lovely served with some chutney and there are so many good ones on the market. Whenever you are in any sort of farm shop, look out for homemade chutneys. Decant some into a glass dish and serve it on your cheeseboard with some crackers.

Red apples, russets or coxes look wonderful in a fabulous old kitchen bowl and require zero talent in the kitchen.

What to serve with cheese

There are all sorts of other treats you can offer with cheese. Be picky about your bread – it doesn't have to be a baguette. Raisin and nut bread is really good with cheese and so is any rustic loaf. I don't think you can beat oatcakes for serving with cheese, the rougher and more homemade the better, and these are much easier to find now.

Muscat raisins and muscat grapes are also delicious with cheese, as are good pears or some quince cheese (often called by its Spanish name, *membrillo*). In the autumn, just put a bowl of apples on the table with your cheese. This is perfect culinary trickery – red apples, russets or coxes, look wonderful in a fabulous old kitchen bowl and require zero talent in the kitchen. When you do this, be confident and don't serve anything else, like salad or crackers. It just gets too confusing and is more work for you.

Otherwise, I recommend serving salad with your cheese course, but keep it simple. Acorn lettuce with some walnuts and a little oil is perfect, particularly with some goat's cheese. Or there is nothing wrong with the heart of an ordinary round lettuce. Your choice of salad depends slightly on the cheese. I had a soft creamy cheese the other day with a herby salad, which was very good. Sometimes those very mild cheeses are helped along a bit by something herby. To dress the salad, grate a little garlic in the bottom of the salad bowl with some olive oil before you add your leaves. This is delicious and you don't need any vinegar.

PACING YOURSELF

It is vital to leave some gaps between courses – dinner can feel like a race if plates are taken away and new ones instantly put in their place. The cheese course can be very handy from your point of view. At this stage, there is a good chatter going on and no one will mind if you disappear from the table for a while to get pudding or coffee ready.

CHAOS IN THE KITCHEN

Quite honestly, you aren't human unless there is a little chaos in the kitchen at some point in the proceedings. Whether it comes before, during or at some stage towards the end of the evening, don't panic about it. You have to face disasters head on. A little chaos is a good thing; it is better if it happens before but it is as likely to happen during.

If you have really ruined the main course and it is too late to do anything about it then you have a few options open to you. Firstly don't struggle on with it, always declare disasters. Then amalgamate your cheese course with the rest of your main course, so do something like cheese and salad with potatoes and the rest of the vegetables. Or call for a takeaway, or look in the fridge and make scrambled eggs for everyone. The truth is that people don't really mind a disaster – they are actually quite entertained by it – but what they can't tolerate is being forced to eat a burnt dinner, pretending that it is delicious, while the hostess is trying (and failing) to mask her desperation over her ghastly dinner party that is falling apart around her ankles.

WAITING FOR STRAGGLING GUESTS

If you ask people for 8.30 it can be about 9.30 before you sit down to dinner. And if your friends are anything like mine they will be late. But I don't think that you can hold dinner off much later than 9.30 and if you are still waiting for people at that time, start heading towards the table. They will probably arrive at any minute and if they don't, it's their problem not yours. You don't want to let meat or vegetables ruin because someone is late.

Remember that most meat benefits from sitting before it is eaten, so you can buy yourself some time there, but there is really nothing more annoying than it being ruined by tardy guests. This is another reason why you don't want to create too much work for yourself, or you will be red-faced and generally harassed and then really upset when the meat tastes of old shoe leather because it's been kept warm too long. Go ahead and eat and everyone will have a better time. The latecomers might be a little embarrassed when they arrive, but that is a lot better than you being visibly harassed and upset, and your guests hungry and treading on eggshells so as not to upset you more.

THANK YOU LETTERS

Thank you letters are not always necessary. I think that you should concentrate on writing them to the people that care about them. For good friends you will want to call after a dinner, which is much more fun for both of you as you can have a good old rake over the evening.

A good barometer of whether a thank you letter is necessary is if there has been a placement or not. When a party has taken a lot of plotting, planning, time, effort then you really need to write. This is because when you have put that much into an evening you want to hear that it was enjoyed.

Competitive thank you letters are very dull. There is no need to write pages and pages about an event – after all, your host was there too, remember. Always include some news, either from the party or not. If you have some good party gossip then include it; that is the best.

The time that you really have to write is when you have been given a present. There is nothing worse than leaving a present for someone at their birthday and never hearing from them. One has usually taken a lot of care over it and silence is the worst sort of response.

Flowers the next day is the loveliest way to thank someone. It is quite a grand thing to do, so is really not really necessary but if someone has given a dinner for you then this is a lovely way to show that you appreciate it. If you do this and you are able, the final great detail is to have a note handwritten by you attached to the bunch, rather than a mispelt card done by the florist.

To be honest, I think that after you have been to someone's house for dinner, word that you had a good time is great however it gets there. Text, email, letter or call – any of these are good. Don't get sniffy about the minutiae.

WHEN A PARTY HAS TAKEN A LOT OF PLOTTING, PLANNING, TIME, EFFORT THEN YOU REALLY NEED TO WRITE.

COOKING FOR CHILDREN

Organic
Cola

COOKING FOR CHILDREN

I don't have any children, so my experience is all to do with spoiling other people's, which I highly recommend. Treats are the easiest way to a child's heart so if you're expecting little visitors, get some goodies and offer something as soon as they enter your house. Fizzy drinks and chocolate are the fastest ways to a child's heart. A lollipop in your pocket is quite a handy thing too. This is best when they are not usually allowed such sugary treats. Go easily with them, because there is a reason you will discover that parents are not keen on too much sugar – it can turn the most adorable children in to the most intolerable monsters. Of course, other people's children go home eventually so the problem is limited, but if you like your friends then you probably won't want to give them a nightmare evening.

Small children will be very happy with a small amount of fizzy drink if you give it to them in a good, but small, glass. After all, no one wants a glass that is a quarter full of anything – I used to hate that as a child – and if they have a little glass filled to the top they won't even notice the small amount. Or you can get mini-cans of fizzy drinks like they have on aeroplanes and these are the perfect size for little hands. Most things come in mini versions now, including delicious ice creams and chocolate bars, which grown-ups like me love, too. Treats for children need to be small, naughty and good to look at as children are so visual.

MILKY DRINKS

If sugary drinks are not allowed you can wow children with milk froth, especially if you're having coffee too. You will need a latte whip. Warm some milk (make sure it doesn't get too hot), froth it until it is thick like cream, then pour the froth into a tiny bowl or small mug. I have always had great success with this and parents approve too, which isn't often the case with my treats. You really must be careful, though, that the milk isn't hot – I speak from experience. Stick your finger in and test the milk before the visiting little angel sticks its tongue in and screams the place down.

Pink milk is one of my favourite things to serve children. Put a few drops of food colouring in some milk and children will think you are rather exciting: knowing a pink cow is going to win you points. My friend Charles says his favourite was peppermint milk – just mix a little peppermint syrup into some milk. Look for peppermint syrup in specialist shops, or use peppermint essence, which is in the baking aisle of most supermarkets. Do check before giving children these drinks though, because some don't like unusual things. I once bought my godson some tablets that turn your bathwater red, blue or green and he was absolutely horrified.

If you are going to make hot chocolate for children then you definitely need to go and get some mini-marshmallows for the top, and some grated chocolate. You need it to be very chocolatey and you must use warm, frothy milk. This is why it is really essential to have a latte whisk in your kitchen – I travel with mine. The best hot chocolate is made by melting bars of 70 per cent chocolate. It is a bit of a palaver, but I would say that it is worth it. You can always use powder otherwise, and the best is Suchard Express (reassuringly sweet and hard to get hold of), and after that there is nothing wrong with ordinary stuff. What is totally unforgivable, though, is to make hot chocolate with that powder that you add hot water to; it is revolting and just not worth the calories.

FOOD FOR CHILDREN

Food for visiting children should be small and needs to feel a bit naughty. There will always be tricky eater who only eats baked beans, and if I were you I would leave them to it, provided they are not your children. Just be grateful that you don't have to get involved. Otherwise you can have fun making things for children.

Breakfast

My friend Lucy does a first course for dinner parties

that she calls mini-breakfast and this can also be a fun breakfast – or even tea – for children. She makes mini-fried eggs or a mini-boiled eggs with quails' eggs, fries some little slices of pancetta and some cherry tomatoes, and then makes mini-triangles of fried bread. I know it may sound extravagant to give children quails' eggs, but this is a special treat. And if you don't have your own children, you might like to do this sort of thing once in a while for little visitors. Boiled eggs of any kind seem to be a pretty good all-round hit with children, in my experience. If you over-boil the egg, which is a risk I always run, just chop it up in a bowl with butter. (For direction on boiled eggs, see page 60–1.)

Lunch

Follow the 'mini' rule again, depending on how much time and enthusiasm you have. You could make mini-shepherd's pies in little ramekin dishes and serve mini-vegetables, like baby carrots, with them. You could also buy mini-pots of tomato ketchup, which are really dumpy and sweet. Remember, most children like quite bland foods and really don't like eating anything too adventurous.

Roast chicken with mashed potatoes and peas is the best nursery lunch, and I have found that cutting the chicken into strips makes it much easier for children to eat. They like the strips because they can eat them with their hands and (I'm sure this is the real reason) roast chicken doesn't usually come in strips. I call this bang bang chicken, because the strips look like the bang-bang chicken in Chinese restaurants. I am not sure that with my godson, John, it wasn't the name that made his chicken taste even better. It all really comes down to marketing in the end.

Broccoli seems to be one of those things that parents rather show off about their children liking. Lucy says that really most children like broccoli, but that all parents cannot help themselves from showing off about their children eating vegetables. One way to encourage little girls is to tell them it will make their hair grow long, which apparently has an amazing effect. The good thing about broccoli is that you can cut it to look like trees and stand them up in the mash potatoes. I know that you're not supposed to play with food, but vegetable landscaping is quite fun and this is not a daily event.

Fish and chips is a good lunch. You can get goujons of fish and oven fries in most supermarkets;

serve it in newspaper. Depending on how creative you are feeling you can make a cone of paper filled with chips and stuff it in a tumbler. This can either be served at the table or you can set up a nursery picnic; we used to love picnics on the nursery floor.

Children also like to be left to it. In the summer you can have children eating together in the garden and eating with their fingers out of paper is a pretty happy situation. The same applies with chicken goujons which you can also get ready-prepared.

Pasta with butter and cheese is a pretty safe bet and if you look in delis you can get tiny pasta that is used for soups. I bought some the other day that was in the shape of stars. A plain tomato sauce (see page 28) is usually acceptable to even the blandest palate. With other people's children you really just want to give them food that they are going to eat, and pasta is always quite a sure bet.

Puddings

Get some small, ordinary biscuits, like those delicious malted milk ones that you can buy in any supermarket or grocers. The sort I like are very small and have an imprint of a cow on the side. Wedge some vanilla ice cream between two to make a sandwich. Utterly yummy just like this, but if you want to go one step further, melt some chocolate and put it in a bowl in the middle of the table for everyone to dip their ice cream sandwiches into. Staggeringly simple, but I promise you everyone – children and grown-ups alike – will whoop with delight.

If you fancy it, get a tub of hundreds and thousands and you can do a third dip which will leave your biscuit looking a bit like a Zoom ice lolly. Hundreds and thousands also make the best sandwiches. Sprinkle them over buttered white sliced bread and leave them open. They are so pretty and utterly delicious. No sane parent would give these to their children, which will make them (the children) think that you are amazingly cool, which is of course exactly what one wants.

Parties

A piñata is the essential thing to have for parties; it goes down seriously well. Piñatas are made from papier mâché and come in all different shapes. For Hallowe'en I got a witch on a broomstick for Godson John and Eleanor (both 3 years old; Eleanor is an almost-god daughter – I think we are on the verge of adopting one another). You hang up the piñata and the children take turns to beat it with a stick. Eventually an adult steps in to loosen it up and then, after a lot more bashing, it splits and showers them with sweets and small toys. If you have one of these you don't need anything else.

Teatime

Making a miniature tea is fun and I like looking for mini-cakes and biscuits in the shops. Have little plates and the tiny glasses that you use for espressos or liqueurs, unless the children bring their own plastic cups. Jessie, my old nanny, always maintains that children like small food and this makes perfect sense. Can you imagine being given a sandwich that is three times the size of your hand? It would be horrifying, but that is how a normal sandwich feels to a child. Jessie makes tiny sandwiches, with ham, marmite, cheese, egg or tomato, and cuts the crusts off – delicious and not complicated to make. She also does these adorable things called jam pennies, which are jam sandwiches cut with a cookie cutter to about the size of 10-p piece. The extraordinary thing is that a child might not finish a normal-size sandwich but will eat lots of tiny ones.

Fairy cakes

When we were children we sat down every day to the most amazing tea. Jessie, was legendary for her teas, the stars of which were her sandwiches and fairy cakes. She always cut the crusts off her sandwiches which were usually tomato, cucumber, egg or ham. The tomatoes were always peeled, so were the cucumbers, and the thinnest ham only was used. Then they were cut into quarters. We were very lucky! These are still the best sandwiches I have ever eaten and if I ever find myself having an 'English' tea in one of the big hotels, I am afraid that their sandwiches never really match up. If you have the time delicious sandwiches are very easy to make and I thoroughly recommend it as there is nothing lovelier for everyone, adult or child, than sitting down to a proper tea. Little sausages hot from the oven are delicious, as is a cake or two (which one should always buy – it is quite hard to make a good cake and extremely time-consuming). If you are planning a tea in advance you can nearly always find a frustrated baker who will make you a Victoria sponge, or head to the farmers' market for some flapjacks or cookies. Supermarkets will have baby gems, which, while they are really dry and disgusting, add both colour and nostalgia to the table.

Fairy cakes are the best. Jessie used to make the littlest ones which means that you ended up eating loads of them. But the smaller they are, the prettier they are. Ice them with white or pale pink icing and then Jessie put a smartie on the top. I saw something fantastic the other day which was a chocolate cupcake baked with a marshmallow in the middle. For American cupcakes you can use Betty Crocker cake mixes, which makes those insanely delicious, synthetic-tasting cakes. You can also buy delicious frosting that has that wonderful American 'formica and strip lighting' taste, too. It is so good. Add some sprinkles for good measure.

> THERE IS NOTHING LOVELIER FOR EVERYONE, ADULT OR CHILD, THAN SITTING DOWN TO A PROPER TEA.

JESSIE'S FAIRY CAKES

4 oz unsalted butter

2 oz caster sugar

6 oz self-raising flour

1 egg

1 teaspoon of vanilla essence

1 teaspoon of milk

- Cream the sugar and the butter.
- In a separate bowl beat the egg with the vanilla essence.
- Add the beaten egg to the creamed butter and sugar and stir.
- Fold in the flour.
- Add the milk.
- Put into little petit fours cases and in a fairly hot oven (gas mark 7 or 200°C) for 7–8 minutes, depending on your oven.
- When they have cooled ice them with white or pale-pink icing and add a Smartie to the top of each one.

CELEBRATIONS

CELEBRATIONS

There are times when we want to throw a party or get together with friends because there is something to celebrate, and other times when we look for a celebration as an excuse to have a party. I have found myself looking for reasons to celebrate before now, and you can find some pretty good ones on any calendar.

The first day of autumn appeals to me as a reason for a party. The new season can be exciting and autumn is a good time to meet up again with friends post-holidays. The first day of spring is just as good, as is midsummer, and there are so many occasions to celebrate in winter – Halloween, Thanksgiving, Christmas, the festival of lights, to name a few.

A seasonal party is easy to theme and, while I am not always a big fan of theming, it can be good to have an anchor for your evening. For example, leaves are an obvious theme for an autumn party. You could serve stuffed vine leaves, although it's impossible even to entertain the idea of making them. Call your local Turkish or Lebanese and get takeaway. To follow, you could have a big bowl of delicious spaghetti with garlic, chilli and bacon, all the right sort of autumn colours, then some salad and cheese. Use acorn lettuce if you can find it, as the leaves are reddish-brown and green and look like oak leaves, and lay your cheeses out on autumn leaves. For a spring party, you could have huge vases full of blossom-laden branches on the table and serve lots of delicious spring vegetables and bowls of cherries.

In some countries people celebrate their name days. I remember feeling envious of my best friend at primary school who was Greek and used to get a present on her name day. Anyone with a saint's name will have a name day, and while you may not want to encourage children to demand more presents, it could be fun to give them a special tea.

PERSONAL CELEBRATIONS

Then there are more personal causes for celebration such as birthdays and special successes that warrant a celebratory dinner. It is worth looking out for such events because they can come and go in people's lives without comment, and it's usually up to someone else to notice them. After all, it's not always easy to announce that you have just done something spectacularly clever and you want to celebrate it, but if someone else recognises what you have done and suggests a party – well, what a treat and how exciting. In fact, I think we should stop hanging around waiting for other people and announce our own achievements and reasons to celebrate. Celebrations are a great way to entertain – they create a good atmosphere and there is nothing cheerier than friends around the table to toast another friend's achievement. These dinners can be relatively simple but they do need something that is sparkly or slightly extravagant.

The last time I threw a celebratory dinner was for my friend Glen. He had just finished making a film that had taken an awfully long time. He'd been working abroad, so the film's completion also meant he was coming home – another reason for celebration. We planned dinner for six at my house and tried to think what would be Glen's favourite dinner – it's important to have the guest of honour's favourites rather than your own. Glen loves Japanese food, so I headed for a Japanese restaurant for takeaway.

If you are going to go the take-out route, you have to do certain things right, like go to a good place, choose things that can travel (for example, avoid tempura which will be soggy and nasty by the time you get it home), and make sure that you've got rid of all the foil containers before anyone arrives. To be honest, the very fact that you have got together a group of people in honour of someone is 95 per cent of what is going to make the evening a success.

ST VALENTINE'S DAY

This can be a tricky day. I, for one, don't especially revel in the idea of being one of the suckers at a table for two in a restaurant somewhere. And if you're not in love, Valentine's Day can turn into one of those green and hairy nights, when you feel that the entire rest of the world is snuggled up having a lovely time. So the best

thing to do is celebrate with a group of people, most of whom will be hugely relieved to be offered a way out of twosomes or lonesomes, so you can buy into the day with merriment.

If you want to be romantic, I think Valentine's is best celebrated at breakfast, exchanging presents and tucking into heart-shaped eggs. There are several ways of making these: you can buy little frying pans that have a mould in the middle in the shape of a heart or you can put a heart-shaped cookie cutter in your normal pan. Or you can cut heart-shaped bread and trim the egg to fit. A heart-shaped cookie cutter is key to this breakfast because you can cut everything. I love brown heart-shaped toast with raspberry jam.

Another idea is to have red fruits. I know February is not the easiest time of year for fruit, but you can usually find redcurrants or raspberries, and if you feel at all inclined to do some cooking you could make your own compôte to serve with pancakes or porridge.

Compote

My friend Gail , who runs a wonderful deli in London, makes this delicious compôte. It is the most perfect bright red, just right for Valentine's morning. Put the fruit in a pan with half its weight in sugar and simmer gently for half an hour (see also page 105). Don't cook it fast or the colour goes. You can make this compôte/jam with any seasonal fruit that you like, but cranberries or redcurrants are ideal for St Val's, and you can get frozen raspberries very easily.

A Valentine's Day breakfast table or tray is fun to lay. You could use large red polkadot handkerchiefs as napkins, or red and white gingham. These would look lovely with wooden bowls, especially if you are having porridge and compôte – quite Swiss looking. If you are ever in Switzerland or the Alps, look out for toast racks and other table things made from wood with hearts carved into them – so pretty.

Or you might prefer a lighter look. Look for napkins with hearts embroidered on them. You only need two for a romantic breakfast, which makes this extravagance slightly more affordable. Just before Valentine's Day, you often see special things like heart-in the shops, and if you buy well, these are things that you will want to use the rest of the year. Little ceramic or glass heart-shaped dishes also look lovely filled with butter or pink sugar.

If you have children, breakfast will obviously be at the table, not on a romantic-looking tray. It's still fun to celebrate, and lovely for the children to come down to breakfast and find heart-shaped toast or pancakes – a cheery start to the day in the middle of an otherwise dreary month.

If you want to be romantic, I think Valentine's is best celebrated at breakfast, exchanging presents and tucking into heart-shaped eggs.

Caviar

I feel I have to mention caviar. I know it is wildly impractical of me but it is a perfect Valentine's treat. It is also the ultimate fast food and requires nothing more than opening a tin and applying a horn spoon. There's no point in having caviar if you can't have as much as you want. So . . . eat it alone or with one other. If caviar is something you really, really love and you have something very special you want to celebrate, then you find a way to afford it. You just have to sacrifice other things. Your dinner may have to be for two or four instead of eight or twelve and you may have to eat at home instead of going out. After all, you can very easily spend £50 a head in a restaurant on a special dinner, or you could buy a 250-gram pot of sevruga caviar for about £130. This would feed four people generously and two people really piggishly, which is what a celebration is all about.

Serving caviar is about presentation, not cooking. Have lots of crisp linen to hand and sit the tin of caviar in a beautiful glass bowl of ice. Keep everything around it pretty and delicate, as caviar is a delicate thing itself. Have very cold vodka in tiny glasses and serve blinis, little pancakes which cost next to nothing, or baked potatoes, which also cost almost nothing and take little brain power to cook (see page 26–7). Add lemons and crème fraîche or simply a horn or mother-of-pearl spoon for spooning the stuff straight into your mouth. This is a special treat and can be very romantic.

Lobsters

These are another special treat, either as part of a feast or as a delicacy. Either way, eating them can become quite raucous – and fun – because you have to dive in with your hands. If you are on almost any cold-water coast you will be able to buy lobsters relatively easily and they are the perfect thing for a celebration – and a little culinary trickery. If bought cooked and cold, no cooking is required and they are best served simply with some mayonnaise, new potatoes and salad.

MOTHER'S DAY

This is such a lovely day and seems to mark the beginning of spring, with its tradition of floral gifts. I always think of Mother's Day as a Sunday lunch celebration. I cannot imagine anything nicer than a long table covered with a white damask cloth and lined with unruly bunches or pots of narcissi. As it is springtime, I like to serve roast lamb – one of the easiest things to make and utterly delicious, provided you don't overcook it (see pages 138–140). If you don't want to do lamb, there's nothing wrong with that old faithful – golden roast chicken (see pages 142–5).

Keep things light. New potatoes are perfect at this time of year and are good boiled, or roasted in a baking tray with olive oil and garlic. Depending on how confident you feel, you could make a big mixed salad or a green vegetable. If you do a salad, keep it green with mixed leaves and a lot of herbs, especially mint. If you want to have a hot vegetable, fresh peas with butter and mint are just right. You could also try broad beans or Brussels sprouts, but both are quite time–consuming in their preparation. Brussels sprouts need to be served straight out of the pan or they go dark green and become not at all appealing. You want to keep them that zinging green colour.

If you're cooking vegetables, do potatoes in the oven. I find trying to boil lots of vegetables totally stressful, because they so easily overcook. The joy of a roasted potato is that it doesn't mind staying in the oven for a little longer – like an easy-going friend who doesn't mind waiting for you. In fact, it gets more delicious.

Pudding

The great thing about Sunday lunch celebrations is that you can serve a pudding. People have room for pudding at lunch and as it's Sunday you will probably have time to buy or make one. Even non-cooks like to make puddings – they're much more enticing than anything else I think, and good to serve. This is the perfect time for an orange Passover cake served with crème fraiche or carrot cake (pages 216–19). My other favourite puddings are bread and butter pudding (pages 240–3) – not light, but yummy, and you can make it the day before – and cheesecake, which is a fairly unexpected pudding in England so scores extra points with me.

Have some shortbread or something handy for a tea tray later on in the day for anyone who stays on into the afternoon. This is a day that should be lingered over and enjoyed and a tea tray is a rare treat. For tea-time and tea-tray ideas, see pages 101–5.

EVEN NON-COOKS LIKE TO MAKE PUDDINGS – THEY'RE MUCH MORE FUN THAN ANYTHING ELSE, I THINK, AND FUN TO SERVE.

A BUFFET

Some celebrations involve the entire family and many friends gathering round a huge table. It is times like these that you need to use everything – your own culinary skills and tricks and everyone else's. I think this is the recipe for the best kind of celebration, partly because if everyone is involved, everyone has a good time. I am not usually a big fan of the buffet, but this is definitely the moment for it. If you can host the celebration outside, then so much the better. In winter you just have to push the furniture back.

The groaning table

Sometimes it's right that the buffet table is groaning with food. After all, buffets are like indoor picnics, and on picnics I like the feeling that the choices are never-ending. The work that goes into a table weighed down with a million choices is beyond my comprehension and I know that if I attempted such a thing I would be half dead by the time anyone arrived and certainly not remotely pleased to see them. But there is a way. And that is to enlist everyone's help. There is something lovely about the kind of celebration when everyone pitches in and arrives with their dish. They should also leave with their dish and any leftovers.

What you need to do is sit down, probably with a couple of other people, and work out where everyone's expertise lies and arrange who's bringing what. This is important so you don't end up with 35 puddings and one rice salad. If you are clever, you could delegate so well that you don't have to cook anything.

If you feel it is getting complicated, just stop, reel in and simplify. The point of the event is for everyone to be together. Just make sure there is enough to drink and Great-aunt Aggie is comfy in the corner with a pink gin, and all should be well.

A ham is a good choice for a simple buffet and delicious at any time of the year, winter or summer. You can buy a whole cooked ham from your butcher, although it is not a hard thing to do yourself. Or you could roast a few chickens (depending on how many people there are going to be) and serve them at room temperature. You don't have to carve them in the traditional Sunday roast way – just cut them up and put them on a platter like they do in France.

IF YOU FEEL IT IS GETTING COMPLICATED, JUST STOP, REEL IN AND SIMPLIFY. THE POINT OF THE EVENT IS FOR EVERYONE TO BE TOGETHER.

Salads

Then you need salads – three is a good number, I think. One of my current favourites is cos lettuce with some crumbled feta cheese, which is yummy and very easy. Also popular is coronation chicken – one of my all-time favourite things as long as it doesn't have scary bits of walnuts and apple – and dishes of rice. Just don't do bog-standard white rice. Organic brown rice or wild rice is a good culinary trick, as it looks and tastes different although it cooks in the same way as ordinary rice but takes longer. You can make a delicious wild rice salad by adding broad beans. If you really feel you can't cope, most delis do a good rice salad.

I went to talk to Gail Stevens about the salads she sells at Baker and Spice. Her food lends itself fantastically well to buffets. One I particularly love is her wild rice and broad bean salad. It is so beautiful to look at that you just have to eat it – this is the sort of food you want to be serving. Gail creates dishes by appearance: she may be inspired by the colours in a bunch of flowers and will mentally translate the colours into ingredients. For this rice salad, she combines the brown of the rice with very sharp green (a palette that appeals to me enormously). The green comes from the broad beans (one of my favourite things), baby spinach leaves and chives. There are also some butter beans in there and, for added colour and zest, pomegranate kernels when they are in season (which is from about September/October to January/February).

Gail's wild rice salad

Cook some organic wild rice. It takes ages, about 45 minutes. When it is done, rinse it thoroughly under cold water to cool it down and stop it continuing to cook. Drain it very well – you don't want water lurking at the bottom of your salad bowl. Use fresh or frozen broad beans depending on the time of year. If you have fresh, pod them and plunge them into boiling water for two minutes. Drain and rinse them under very cold water to stop them from cooking any more. This also keeps their colour that vibrant green. When they're cool, remove the tough outer skins from each bean. This takes a while, but you get the hang of it pretty quickly. I find that if I nick one end with my nail and squeeze gently, the bean just pops out. You really should do this as the beans taste much better without their skins, and by the end of the season it's essential, as the skins get quite tough. If you are using frozen, your job is much easier and you can't really tell the difference, especially in a salad. Gail uses frozen beans in the winter so they must be fine. All you have to do is defrost them and remove the tough skins. You don't even have to cook them because the freezing process has broken down the cellulose, in effect cooking them.

Take a tin of butterbeans and rinse them thoroughly under the cold tap. When the rice is cool, mix it with the butterbeans and the shelled broad beans. Add the pomegranate kernels – when they are out of season you can use toasted pumpkin seeds if you like – and at the last minute, add the baby spinach and chopped chives. Gail simply dresses this salad with olive oil and salt and pepper – no acid like vinegar or lemon juice because it would discolour the beans. The point of this salad is its wonderful colour and it really doesn't need the lemon juice.

This is exactly how Gail gave me the recipe. Quantities are up to you, but you will need quite a lot of broad beans. You can prepare the beans for this salad a maximum of 24 hours in advance and once you have done that, all you have to do is cook the rice, and the rest is pretty instant. Be careful not to over-dress the salad – the oil should just glaze the rice and not be too obvious. Too much dressing weighs salads down – that is a key point and something to remember generally.

The starting point for this salad is that rice and beans are an excellent combination, found in many recipes from all over the world. This is a good guide, and funnily enough one that I use in decorating. You can often take something that is quite commonplace and make something good by just upping the quality and altering the style. This rice salad is exactly that. Think of the rice and kidney bean salad that was so popular in the seventies – this is just a re-working. If you try to think like this, lots of ideas will start to come to you.

THERE IS SOMETHING LOVELY ABOUT THE KIND OF CELEBRATION WHEN EVERYONE PITCHES IN AND ARRIVES WITH THEIR DISH. THEY SHOULD ALSO LEAVE WITH THEIR DISH AND ANY LEFTOVERS.

Potato salads

Most people love potato salad and I don't think that a buffet is complete without it. Gail's version is served warm, although you can serve it cold. The key thing I have learnt is that you have to start with hot potatoes. It's no good chopping up cold leftover potatoes and turning them into a salad. Gail recommends new or waxy potatoes (Nicola or Charlotte), but you can use any of the many salad potatoes on the market.

To make the salad, boil the potatoes, peel them if you want to and cut them in half. The dressing is made with warm honey and some olive oil and lemon juice. I used the juice of half a lemon and two tablespoons of honey, which I warmed in a pan. I added a generous tablespoon of olive oil and some salt and pepper. It took precisely 30 seconds and I feel like a genius. In fact you are jolly lucky I am sharing this with you, as I would quite like to keep it to myself for a while. You can add some roughly chopped coriander (if you like it; I don't) or flat-leaf parsley or a combination of the two. Add some sliced spring onions and chopped red onion to the dressing – vital for their wonderful colour and flavour – pour everything over the potatoes and mix well. The dressing must be warm (not boiling or simmering) when it goes on. It's best to mix the salad in a big bowl then transfer it to a beautiful platter to serve. The bowl you mix the salad in will look all messy and greasy by the time you've finished with it. Serve this salad warm or at room temperature. See pages 29–31, 37, 145, 148 and 258 for more about dressing and tossing salads.

Hot roasted butternut squash

This is the final dish that Gail suggested. Perfect for a winter buffet when you want something hot, and it adds wonderful colour. First of all turn the oven on to get piping hot (250°C/gas mark 8). Peel the butternut squash and chop into bite-size pieces. Put them in a mixing bowl and toss with olive oil, chopped fresh sage, salt and pepper. Transfer onto a baking tray and sling in the oven for the 10–20 minutes, depending on the heat of your oven and the size of your pieces of squash.

Baked potatoes

These are really easy to make (see pages 26–7) and work both winter and summer. A big basket of them on the table looks good and everyone loves them. Serve some cold meat and one salad alongside and everyone will be happy, as long as you have enough butter and salt.

If you can, get hold of some fancy butter. These little details are what culinary trickery is all about. You can sometimes find hand-rolled pats of butter with stamps of cows on in specialist shops or organic farm shops, and I've seen huge pats from which they cut pieces like little cheeses. It might be difficult to find, but on the table it will look simple and show such flair. An alternative is to get commercial-size pats and cut big hunks of butter from them to put on the table. For this you might have to sidle up to a local restaurant or deli and see if they will sell you one from their own order. Charm is all you need and if you are giving some sort of party you will probably need to buy some stuff from them anyway, which will – yes – butter them up nicely!

The cheeses

I think one large cheese, such as a Stilton, Cheddar or Brie, looks lovely on a buffet. Apart from anything else, it makes life so simple. I always offer salad with cheese, especially now that there are so many people on no-wheat diets, but bread or some good oatcakes go down well too. With a buffet, you have space to put some quince cheese on the table or some sort of chutney that is good with cheese. Pickled walnuts are also good. Specialist cheese shops usually have endless extra treats for serving with cheese, such as dates and Muscat raisins still on their branches, which look beautiful and taste so good. The raisins on the branch are rather special, but you can buy dates in most supermarkets. Be careful which ones you get. The ones with the loose skins are horrible and remind me of cockroaches – not a good look for any sort of celebration. Look for medjool dates with the tight, glistening skins.

Condiments are the key to a cold buffet

All of these things are easy to find and something that even non-cooks can enjoy buying. While exotic ingredients in a food shop might paralyse you with fear, you can cope with mustards and chutneys. I am a big fan of beet and horseradish sauce, which is ideal for a buffet. Not only does it taste wonderful, but the colour is glorious and a bowl of it looks very perky.

A simpler table

You don't always need to do the huge groaning buffet thing. I sometimes find them overwhelming and can't decide what to have, so end up with a really weird collection of things on my plate. I went to a friend's cocktail party recently and they had the smartest buffet I've ever seen. On the table was a big piece of roast beef with a bowl of horseradish, rocket salad, a whole brie and two huge round loaves of bread – beef sandwiches for anyone who wanted. It was delicious and showed such style. This is also foolproof – you just have to be careful not to overcook the beef (see pages 137–8 for more information) and to cut it quite thinly. If you buy a really good piece of meat you will probably still only spend the same, or even less money, than if you faffed about with loads of different things. A meal like this has the bonus of there being relatively little washing up and chaos in the kitchen once you have made it and you won't be eating weird leftovers for the rest of the week.

Hot buffet dishes

The other problem with too much food at buffets is that you are usually eating off your lap and it's hard to cut food when there is no table – another reason to keep things simple. In winter, things like lasagne or shepherd's pie are loved by almost everyone and they can be eaten with just a fork, which is a bonus If you live in a town or city you will probably have a good deli that would make a lasagne for you, and if you order in advance, I bet they would make it in one of your own dishes. This is one of the great culinary tricks and I highly recommend it. Shepherd's pie, however, is not hard to make yourself. My mother can't cook, but she makes a very good shepherd's pie.

YOU DON'T ALWAYS NEED TO DO THE HUGE GROANING BUFFET THING. I SOMETIMES FIND THEM OVERWHELMING AND CAN'T DECIDE WHAT TO HAVE, SO END UP WITH A REALLY WEIRD COLLECTION OF THINGS ON MY PLATE.

MY MOTHER'S SHEPHERD'S PIE (MADE FROM SCRATCH)

olive oil
onions, chopped
best-quality minced lamb
1 tin Italian peeled tomatoes
Worcester sauce
tomato ketchup
salt and black pepper
potatoes

- Pour a little olive oil into a pan and 'sweat' the onions. This means cook them until they are soft and transparent, but not brown.
- Add the lamb to the pan, turning it with a wooden spoon until it has lost its raw look and is slightly brown.
- Add the tin of tomatoes and liberally season with Worcester sauce and ketchup. Cook over a low heat until the lamb is cooked and brown – keep stirring so the mince doesn't form lumps.
- Take off the heat and allow to cool.
- Once it's cool, remove all traces of fat from the top of the lamb. Using a draining spoon, transfer the meat into a baking dish, with only a little of the sauce.
- Bake masses of large potatoes in the oven. When they are well cooked, scoop out all fluffy insides and mash with salt and butter. Add to the top of the mince. Now you can either freeze this for future events or dot the potato with butter and bake in a pre-heated oven until well browned and piping hot.

JANE'S SHEPHERD'S PIE (MADE FROM LEFTOVERS)

Jane, my fairy godmother, makes what she says herself is the best shepherd's pie. She says it is so good that she could sit in it – that's pretty good. This is Jane's way:

- Toss any roast lamb left over from Sunday lunch into the food processor and whizz it briefly to mince it.
- Put this into a dish, add some mashed potatoes on the top and pop it in the oven to heat through and brown.

I have watched Jane do this and it really does take her half a second, which is a bit disappointing. I felt like asking her if she could try and make it look a bit more complicated. This is an excellent supper for a Monday night after the Sunday roast. I don't tend to have leftovers handy, because you have to be in a lot for that, and have people around that are going to eat them, but if you do, this is just perfect.

By the way, cottage pie is made with beef, and people have quite strong views about whether they like to have theirs with beef or lamb.

Serving shepherd's pie

When my mum served shepherd's pie at my sister's birthday she put mini-bottles of ketchup at everyone's place, which looked so pretty. You can't eat shepherd's pie without ketchup and bowls of it look so silly. If you can't locate the mini-bottles, just put bottles of ketchup, mustard and Worcester sauce on the table. My friend Honor insists that adding sweetcorn really makes a shepherd's pie and adds succulence, although she does admit it looks a bit dodgy. If you don't want to add sweetcorn to your pie you could always serve a bowl of it as one of the vegetables, along with peas. I used to work with someone who put all the vegetables – chunks of carrot and broccoli – into the pie while he was making it, which was delicious. Once you have started to cook this and got used to it, you can make it your dish and cook it by taste rather than by the recipe. If you are making it with beef instead of lamb you could also add some horseradish to your mash (see page 150).

IN WINTER, DISHES LIKE LASAGNE OR SHEPHERD'S PIE ARE LOVED BY ALMOST EVERYONE AND THEY CAN BE EATEN WITH A FORK, WHICH IS A BONUS.

Gulls Eggs

EATING OUTDOORS

EATING OUTDOORS

People generally make less of an effort with the table when they are eating outside, but, in fact, this is the time when it is really fun to fuss. When people sit down at a beautifully laid table in the garden on a glorious sunny afternoon, you are at least three-quarters of the way to giving them a really good lunch, and you haven't produced any food yet.

I am much keener on using tablecloths outside than indoors. Outside tables are generally not as nice as those indoors and so benefit from being covered. I am a huge fan of the antique heavy linen sheets you find in France. They make wonderful tablecloths and their flaxy colour is really smart. Equally great are highly starched damask cloths – a little grandeur in the open air is a lot less stuffy than it is indoors. I also like the idea of a patchwork tablecloth, made from vintage napkins. Buy them up (cheaply) and stitch them together with a good coloured thread. Make sure that the dye won't run when washed. Jugs or vases of flowers on outdoor tables look pretty, particularly because you don't expect them outside.

It doesn't matter how haphazard an outdoor table is. If you are totally unprepared and have no outdoor furniture, simply take the dining-room furniture outside, or find an old trestle table with benches and add some big, juicy cushions. The advantage of a trestle is that it is so mobile and can be taken down to the end of a garden or into a field and put under the shade of a big tree – if everyone is prepared to carry the lunch down there too.

Shade, from a tree or a big umbrella, is very important when you are eating outside. Some people like to sit in the sun, but children shouldn't sit in the direct sunlight, and I begin to feel faint just looking at a table without shade. If you can't offer a tree or umbrella, put hats on the table instead. I like a bit of shade in the evening, too; the night sky can seem awfully big and being under a tree gives you a little protection.

Eating outdoors at night

For dinner on the terrace all the same principles apply, but you need some light. Nightlights floating in some water in little jars or tumblers look pretty, and candelabras or candlesticks are wonderful on a very still night. Hurricane shades are the obvious answer, but they do take up a lot of space. Vases can double as hurricane shades and different shapes and colours along a table look great. Hang lanterns in the trees, or get those coloured lightbulbs on garlands and hang them all around the garden with bunting for the ultimate English festive garden.

YOU CAN NOW FIND QUITE EASILY SMALL CANS THAT YOU CAN HANG IN A TREE WITH LIGHTS IN THEM. THEY ARE SO PRETTY AND MAKE A GARDEN LOOK DIVINE.

Summer drinks

Any summer lunch needs lots of ice and refreshing drinks. Pink champagne or prosecco served in tumblers on the rocks is delicious on a hot day, as are Bellinis (see pages 123–124). White wine shandy – white wine and lemonade – sounds weird and slightly disgusting I know, but give it a try; it's actually very good served in jugs with ice and lemon. You could also have traditional shandies – unexpected but so refreshing – and you can have bottles of beer on ice as well. I was offered shandy once at a very smart lunch in Madrid, and suddenly shandies were catapulted from a slightly nasty pub drink to something rather stylish.

For non-alcoholic drinks there is lots of choice. Look in the larger supermarkets or even the all-night grocers and you will find bottles of wonderful lemonade, raspberry and pear juice, and endless nectars such as lychee, which are delicious with some lemonade, mint and ice. Recently I had pomegranate juice with soda water – deeelish, and a beautiful colour. Slightly harder to find, but worth knowing about because it is very refreshing, is almond milk. I first had it in Italy, but you can generally find it in health-food shops now.

Of course the way you serve a drink is half the joy of having one. A table set up as a bar outside with a damask cloth is very good and ice buckets are essential. If you don't have a champagne bucket to put your bottle of wine in, then improvise. You could use an old enamel bucket, or old iron basins are great for keeping things cool. The key thing is ice, and lots of it – those plastic wine coolers don't do it for me.

HOME MADE
LEMONADE

Summer lunch

Serve some baked potatoes, cold roast beef and a couple of good salads (see pages 29–31, 145, 148, 158, 189–193) and you will be championed as having offered a great lunch. If your table is large enough, just put platters down the centre so people can help themselves. This helps the atmosphere round the table, especially if there are quite a few people who don't know each other, as it forces them to talk to one another.

Using the garden in the bleak midwinter

I have to admit that I do feel a bit chilly just thinking about parties outside in winter, but there are times, like bonfire night, when you want to celebrate in the garden. Decorating the garden for winter celebrations is fun. The major plus, of course, is that it gets dark early so you can take full advantage of candlelight and lanterns.

Provided it isn't raining – a pretty big provided – there is no reason why you shouldn't entertain outside. It is easy to rent braziers and, if you get enough of them and your garden isn't too huge, they should keep the place fairly warm. Make sure there are big cushions on all the benches and chairs, and blankets to keep anyone who is sitting down warm. It is also possible to get a city garden or roof terrace tented over with open sides, and you can heat this relatively easy. I have a friend in London who does this every Christmas and it is really quite warm. Provided you give people enough to drink they'll be happy.

Any kind of stew, or the chilli recipe following, would be good served at an outdoor party.

ELLIE'S NEVER-FAIL CHILLI

1kg lean minced beef

I large onion

1 green pepper, diced

1 x 400g tin tomatoes

2–3 tablespoons chilli powder

I teaspoon salt

1/8 teaspoon cayenne pepper

1/8 teaspoon paprika

I x 420g tin kidney beans drained

2 x 225g tins or jars of good tomato sauce

a tablespoon or two of olive oil

- Brown the beef in a little olive oil for 7–10 minutes, then remove from the pan.
- Sauté the onion and green pepper in olive oil.
- Add all the other ingredients and cook for 15 minutes over a low heat. Taste. Add anything else you wish – more seasoning and so on. Let it sit for five minutes or more.

If you want to do something that is thicker and takes more time on the top of the stove, you have to use un-canned dried beans. They take a long time to cook and must be soaked overnight first. Kidney beans must also be boiled briskly in fresh water for at least 15 minutes or they can be toxic. Then add the beef, unbrowned, and everything else. Cook the heck out of it – 4–5 hours at a low temperature – and see if you like that better.

Another good idea for a winter outdoor party is squash and chickpea stew – delicious with wild rice and very warming. I have no idea how to begin making this, but I bought some from a deli recently and sat outside in the cold eating it. If you have a deli or health food shop near you that does that kind of food, ask them. I bet they would make it for you, then all you have to do is heat it up and serve it in large mugs with spoons. Never feel that you have to make anything yourself if there is someone else who knows how to do it. I also think the wild rice here is key. It is much more delicious than the usual white rice.

Serve hot drinks. A bar at one end of the garden with a suitably wrapped-up barman behind it, serving hot wine or hot toddies, is a very good thing. Have some pumpkin or squash soup in scooped-out baby pumpkins or acorn squashes and make sure there are lots of sausages. At these sorts of events people love hamburgers and hot dogs, as well as hot chocolate with mini-marshmallows, which can also be toasted on a bonfire or barbecue.

PICNICS

The British are pretty good at picnics. So good, in fact, that the French have adopted our word for them since they don't seem to have one of their own. And that is saying something, as the French tend to consider all things to do with food their area and certainly not something that we know anything about.

Packing for picnics requires a little skill, none of it necessarily culinary, which is probably why the

French have allowed us to corner this market. There are a few dos and don'ts. I find more dos than don'ts, mercifully. In fact, the only things I think are really dreadful on picnics are pre-packed anything and arriving with a whole load of supermarket shopping bags full of food. So depressing, don't you think? It means no one has lovingly packed the picnic, which is a large part of the point.

Shopping for picnic paraphernalia

Car boot sales, junk shops and antiques markets are all worth investigating for picnic stuff. Thermos flasks have had many style moments. The high-street shops have stylish stainless-steel ones nowadays, or the Chinese ones which are really pretty, but I have a soft spot for the tartan flasks that were *au courant* in the seventies and are now hard to find. You will find old flasks in car boot sales, and if you are really lucky you might discover the type with a cane design on the outside, one of the many style classics to come out of the Thermos factory. For cold drinks, hold on to those bottles with the ceramic and rubber stoppers that fancy lemonade often comes in. You can also find them in junk shops and they are good for decanting homemade lemonade or fruit juices into. It's worth decanting anything that comes in a carton because once opened, cartons can't be closed properly so tend to leak when moved about. Also, glass bottles are much prettier.

Picnic cutlery and plates

For cutlery, I buy up old stuff from the market. There's always plenty available and it doesn't matter if you have a real hotchpotch of different handles and styles. The main thing to avoid is plastic – it is impossible to get anything on to a plastic fork or cut anything with a plastic knife. I really don't see the point of taking plastic as it is not as if you can break normal cutlery and presumably there is no fear of a hijack.

Plates are slightly more difficult, but I do think paper ones are really depressing. I know there are times when they are useful, but eating off something that bends, usually with a plastic knife and fork, is tough on morale, and means whatever you are eating is just that little bit less pleasurable. Paper napkins are never very satisfactory either. I like to take an odd collection of china plates on a picnic, but they do risk getting chipped and broken if they get knocked about too much in the boot of the car. If they are packed tightly enough in a basket they should be OK, though, so don't write this idea off altogether.

Enamel plates are a good alternative and look fabulous in the picnic hamper. They make a proper old clanking noise on the way; I rather like that travelling-tinker racket in the back of the car. You can get most things in enamel – mugs, bowls and plates – and some shops have coloured enamel, which is divinely pretty, especially when it comes in fondant colours. For winter picnics, there are enamel mugs with lids to keep your soup or tea warm and these are equally useful in the summer for keeping the wasps out of your wine. I love drinking wine from enamel mugs on picnics, but I hate those plastic stemmed glasses. Plastic is not good to drink from, ever, and I am not big on metal or silver tumblers either, although they are quite practical.

Packing a picnic

For me, a collection of baskets and large canvas tote bags is the smartest way to carry a picnic. There are also more modern solutions such as a cool box, which makes up for its hideousness by its ability to provide both cold drinks and a seat for anyone who has recently had a hip operation.

Picnics are really about unpacking while everyone is hovering over the basket, waiting to see what comes out. The anticipation is one of your trump cards, so make the most of it. Think of a magician taking a rabbit out of a hat: he doesn't rush but makes a bit of a song and dance about it all. The unwrapping makes the anticipation last a little longer. And if you are anything like me you will enjoy the packing and putting together baskets of things. Think of the crinkle of greaseproof; it will make even the most ordinary pie take on a rather exciting air.

Everything should look as though it has been made at home – it doesn't really have to be, of course, but you do need to re-package. For example, scotch eggs and pork pies are great picnic foods, but unless you are a really keen cook I cannot imagine that you would either know or be interested in how to make either of them. Anyway, they are available in most butchers and supermarkets. Take them out of their horrible plastic

Picnics are really about unpacking while everyone is hovering over the basket. The anticipation is one of your trump cards, so make the most of it.

and polystyrene wrappers and re-wrap in greaseproof or waxed paper tied with string. This will have most people fighting over them and thinking that you are 'a bit of a whiz in the kitchen'. The product has to be good: you will never get away with repackaging some seriously processed pork pie and convince anyone it tastes good; you have to buy well. It is worth going to a good butcher for your pork pies as these are the sorts of things that benefit from being properly made.

Picnic food

For a basic picnic you can't go wrong with a good bap and a large choice of things to put inside it. You can buy baps at most bakers, and if they don't have baps, bread rolls will do. Cold meats are perfect inside your bap, salad (not dressed), and A LOT of mayonnaise, chutneys, salt and pepper. Condiments are key on a picnic and people are overjoyed if you remember the mustard (or furious when you forget it). All good picnics should have an element of leftover about them. Beef from the night before or cold chicken is perfect.

Always remember the 'pic' in picnic and take jars of things to pick at – pickled onions, little gherkins and pickled eggs. Only take pickled eggs if you see a jar with a good label – the market for pickled eggs is almost non-existent now, so the label has probably not been re-designed since the fifties, which makes them worth taking along just to add some charm to your picnic basket. Picnics are really about good shopping. If you are anywhere near a good deli, think about taking a quiche with you or, as they are more fashionably known now, a savoury tart.

Abundance is what you need, and after that you need to be comfortable. A picnic is very much about spending the afternoon lying around, Roman-style, having eaten as much as you possibly can.

A picnic cake

One of the most important things to take on a picnic is a cake. Unless you are good at baking, cakes are hard to do and very time-consuming, so I would strongly recommend buying one. You just have to make sure it has been homemade in someone else's home. If you are in the country, head towards the WI tent at any fête. In town, most bakeries will have something, or persuade your local tea/coffee shop to part with one of their cakes if you are desperate. Whip it into a fabulous old biscuit tin and there you have your homemade cake. Flapjacks, gingerbread – the gooier the better – or chocolate chip cookies are just as good, and farmers' markets are excellent places to look for these types of treats. If you are really stuck and the supermarket is your only option, try to find something you already know is delicious so you're not disappointed, and pop it in your own tin as before.

If shopping for a cake doesn't grab you because you are trying to release your inner-baker, there is a cake I have made and it was delicious. I find it totally impossible to follow a recipe and making cakes is hard, so if I can do it, anyone can. This was sent to me by my best friend's stepmother to start me learning how to cook. There is a slight glitch – you need an electric beater or a KitchenAid mixer. If you don't have anything, borrow something from your mother. If you are as new to cooking as I was when I first made this cake you might need to go shopping before you start. You will need the following equipment:

- two 23cm springform baking tins (springform are the ones with a clip on the side which makes taking the cake out much easier)
- a palette knife – not essential as you can use any old knife if you want
- wire rack for cooling the cake
- packet of wooden skewers
- scales for weighing ingredients
- a cake tin
- an oven timer that rings (it is impossible to remember when to take things out of the oven otherwise)

DIANE'S CARROT CAKE

250g plain flour

2 teaspoons baking powder

1 1/2 teaspoons bicarbonate of soda

1 teaspoon ground cinnamon

1 teaspoon salt

4 large eggs

350g caster sugar

280ml sunflower oil

300g grated carrots (you need to buy more than 300g because by the time you have peeled and topped and tailed them they weigh less than they do in the shop)

FROSTING

200g cream cheese (Philadelphia is good but not that awful lite stuff. At this point it is a bit late for lite anything anyway)

200g unsalted butter

300g icing sugar (golden is good but regular will do. When I first did this I had never heard of golden, but it is right there in the baking section of the supermarket and isn't as hard to find as it sounds)

2 teaspoons pure vanilla extract (a specialist food hall or large supermarket should stock a good one. The Madagascan one is best and you can use it for other things like putting in the top of an espresso)

Take the cream cheese and butter out of the fridge so that they are soft when you come to use them.

DECORATION

You might want to try some of your own style ideas for decorating the cake. I often use crystallized violets on mine, or my friend Diane suggested doing graffiti-style writing with those great tubes of brightly coloured icings you can get in supermarkets.

HOW TO MAKE THE CAKE

- Preheat the oven to 180°C/Gas 4.
- Butter the two 23cm springform tins – the easiest way is to put some butter in your fingertips and rub the tins – then chill them in the fridge.
- Sift the flour, baking powder, bicarbonate of soda, cinnamon and salt into a large bowl.
- Put the eggs in the KitchenAid and whisk at high speed until they are pale and fluffy. If you don't have a KitchenAid, put the eggs in a bowl and beat with an electric whisk.
- Gradually whisk in the sugar and continue whisking until you have a pale and very fluffy mixture. This part can take as long as 5–10 minutes and you really don't want to be doing it manually.
- Add the oil in a thin stream as if you are making mayonnaise. This scared me a bit at first, as I didn't think mayonnaise came in anything other than a jar, but don't be put off. You just have to make sure that it is a very slow stream of oil, otherwise it won't take to the mixture and will curdle – I think. Continue beating all the time. When you are done, the mixture should leave a ribbon trail on itself when you lift the beater.
- Gently fold in the flour mixture and the carrots. Take care not to beat the mixture at this stage or you will loose all the air you have so carefully incorporated into the mix. To fold a mixture, don't stir like you usually would. Just take the spoon right under the mixture and bring it up over the

top, gently combining it. This makes the difference between a light sponge and a brick.

- Divide the mixture between the two tins and pop into the oven for 30–40 minutes. Start testing after 30 minutes. Put a wooden skewer into the centre of each cake. If the skewer comes out clean, whizz the cake out of the oven. If it's sticky with uncooked cake mix, leave for another 5–10 minutes, but test every 5 minutes.
- Once cooked, remove from the oven and turn the cakes out on to a wire rack to cool. Be gentle, the cakes are very fragile at this stage.

When the cake is cold, make the frosting. If you have a KitchenAid mixer, change the whisk from the balloon whisk to the square shaped beater.

- Cream together the cream cheese and the unsalted butter, which should both be out of the fridge and at room temperature.
- Sift in the icing sugar and add the vanilla essence. Whisk together until all the sugar is incorporated into the butter/cheese mix.
- Sandwich the cakes together with frosting and use the rest to cover the top of the cake completely. Use a palette knife if you have one, but a regular knife will do.

It is very important that you don't put this cake in the fridge – the fridge is public enemy number one for all cakes. Put it in the cake tin, keep cool and eat within about five days.

Summer picnics

My idea of a perfect summer picnic is to find a shady spot under a tree (preferably a silver birch) in a wood or by a river and hang out there with friends for most of the afternoon. The great thing about summer picnics is the produce is so good. All you need to do is go to the market in the morning and head into the woods with a grocer's crate of rocket, some juicy ripe tomatoes, a loaf of bread and a bottle of best olive oil. Add some good ham and you are set. A picnic doesn't have to be complicated and when you can buy good raw produce you are much better not to bother doing anything with it. The market will offer you a lot of options for this sort of lunch and you will just have to be strict with yourself about what you take. Think of all the delicious cheeses that any market, anywhere in Europe will have. There may be a stall selling dressed crab or potted shrimps and there is bound to be a charcuterie stand with good salamis and hams. Try not to be tempted to take a bit of everything. If you focus on one or two things you will enjoy them so much more. I have a friend who takes his son to galleries or museums to see one thing. They go in, head straight to the picture or sculpture they are there to see, spend 15 minutes looking at it and then leave. This picnic is a bit like that. There are few opportunities just to enjoy eating something like a hunk of good bread and a delicious tomato, so take full advantage of them when they arise.

You need treats on a picnic and if you are away from home you will usually find there are some pretty good ones among the local produce. Any coastal area will have crab, langoustine and lobsters, and these delectable items are perfect because they don't require much in the way of cutlery (other than some lobster crackers and picks). In fact, they are much better eaten outdoors as they are pretty messy. Is there anything better than sitting on a beach with your jeans rolled up, tucking into lobsters or oysters with some lemons and fresh mayonnaise (for the lobster) and an icy-cold bottle of white wine or Guinness? The thing I love about delicacies like these is that they are either virtually free or really expensive, but they are never better than when eaten on a picnic.

The summer holiday picnic is one of the best. If there are lots of people everyone can bring things and lay out one huge picnic. When I was growing up we used to have lots of these large picnics, when several families would meet halfway up a glen and unload the boots of their cars. I love this and it is a great way to get lots of people together without the strain of eighteen for lunch landing on any one person's shoulders. But it is important that all baskets are opened in the middle of the rug. There is nothing worse than 'ours' and 'theirs' on a picnic; I always get picnic envy – what is standard in someone else's basket is often a novelty in one's own.

Lying around

These big picnics with lots of people are as much about lying around as they are about the lunch. I like to take a large linen sheet with me, because when it is really hot, blankets are not what you want to be lying on and they generally are covered in old grass or even worse, old dog hairs. Linen is extremely easy to wash and can be slung into the washing machine once you are home, which never happens to blankets, adding to their lack of appeal. Having said that, I have just bought a new picnic rug. It is an old Welsh blanket and makes the most lovely picnic rug. The colours are fabulous and the weight of the cloth is nice too – especially when laid on top of the old heavy linen sheets. When we were children we had a tartan blanket backed in waterproof material which was extremely practical on damp ground.

My latest piece of picnic equipment is a piece of MDF to go under the middle of the blanket or sheet. This means you can put the goodies out without them all falling over and everyone can sit round with a solid surface in the middle. I do find it annoying trying to balance jars glasses on uneven ground, and the prettiest areas are usually those where the ground is soft and lumpy. If you find this a step too far, use a tray instead.

I also like to take big square cushions with me on a summer picnic for added comfort, and a thermos of coffee or tea for the afternoon. Remember to take a book with you. Leaning up against a tree reading your book is the best way to spend a summer afternoon. Take a camera, too. You'll find this is a good time to take pictures because people are so relaxed they hardly notice that they are being photographed.

Summer picnic salads

Salads on picnics need to be divided. You need a bag of lettuce for the sandwich makers and a bowl of salad for the non-bread eaters. I am a firm believer that all salads must be dressed, and this rule applies on picnics. Take a jam jar of vinaigrette with you and toss on arrival. Don't do it before you leave or your salad will be like slime by the time you get to eat it.

Salads are the centrepiece of any summery outdoors meal and most need little preparation, particularly now prepared salads are so widely available. I have never been keen on the bags of salad you get at the supermarket, but I have to say that I am beginning to change my mind. I bought one the other day when it was about the only option, and it was very good. Be careful what you choose, though, and avoid ones with lots of iceberg lettuce. The bags with radicchio and lambs lettuce are good and an easy way to make a mixed leaf salad. I get the quantities all wrong when I start buying lots of different lettuces and like to use these bags as a base and add herbs and avocado.

Romaine lettuce is crispy and delicious, as are baby gems. Round lettuce is wonderful, but be prepared to throw away a lot of outside leaves (round lettuce is the cheapest available so this isn't quite as extravagant as it sounds). Endive is good; so are spring onions, tomatoes and avocados. But herbs are the secret to a salad's success. You will be amazed by how many people comment on a salad containing herbs; they make it so tasty. The best herbs to use are dill, basil or mint. Mint is particularly delicious – the Vietnamese use it a lot in their cooking. They make delicious spring rolls wrapped in lettuce leaves with a piece of mint – that's where I got my salad idea.

These big picnics with lots of people are as much about lying around as they are about the lunch.

Tomatoes

I'm not keen on quartered tomatoes, particularly when they are the common English garden variety. They remind me of school salad. Plum, beef and cherry tomatoes are much better. Cherry tomatoes are a bore if they aren't cut in half because they spring off your fork, especially when covered in oil. However, cutting enough of them for lots of people takes ages, so I usually go for plum or beef. I like to cut them in half, scoop out all the core, pips and watery bit with a teaspoon and then rip them up. You can slice if you prefer, but they look rather good ripped. Another good trick is to dunk your tomatoes in boiling water for 30 seconds and then quickly remove the skins with a knife (they slip off). Peeled tomatoes take on an unusual texture and hold dressing very well, so add them as usual to your salad or slice them for a tomato salad with some very finely sliced red onion or spring onion.

Avocados

I spent years avoiding Haas avocados because their skin was so ugly and I could never tell if they were ripe or not. This is one of the times that my 'judge every book by its cover' theory did not pay off. Haas are the best, but their skins are a problem, as you can't peel them easily. The best approach is to take a teaspoon and scoop out the flesh like ice cream. The scoops also look much better in the bowl than the usual chopped-up bits. The ripeness problem is solved now by a lot of the supermarkets having labels that say 'perfectly ripe'.

Spring onions

These are delicious. They can get a bit lost at the bottom of a salad bowl and I find that happens especially when they are chopped in circles. Cut them into strips, like they come with duck pancakes in Chinese restaurants.

I like to be able to eat my salad with a fork only. I think someone once told me you should, but I'm not sure and it doesn't matter anyway. (Just for the record, the same person also told me that it was rude to have seconds of soup.) So I do think that lettuce needs to be chopped and it needs to be crispy or else it is near impossible to get it on your fork. A great deal about cooking (if you can call making a salad cooking, which I, with my limited skills, like to) can be worked out by thinking about how you like to eat it. For dressings and how to toss a salad, see pages 29–31, 37 and 99.

Winter picnics

The winter picnic is an underrated event. I am not usually a fan of striding about the countryside, but taking a picnic is one way to make it more attractive, especially during the winter.

I prefer to eat a winter picnic from the back of a car halfway up a glen, with some dilapidated shack nearby for shelter. When it's really cold you can't stay still for very long, so these picnics are better closer to spring, when there are some slightly warmer days, than in the thick of winter. A brisk day with blue sky and sunshine – that's when you want to grab the picnic rug and head for the hills with hot goodies. Take proper thick rugs so you don't get a damp bottom when you sit down.

I am not usually a fan of striding about the countryside, but taking a picnic is one way to make it more attractive, especially during the winter.

The food on a winter picnic takes some thinking about, so while you are grazing through cookery books keep an eye out for good things. Hot soup with cheese scones is really yummy. Think of gloved hands round enamel mugs of piping hot soup, but it's the scones that get people excited. If you make them just before you go and take them straight from the oven, they should still be warm by the time you eat them. (See pages 228–9 for recipes.) Tomato soup is good because everyone loves it and you can bloody Mary it up a bit on cold days. Hot bloody bull shots – bloody Mary with beef consommé – are good too (see page 125).

Little hot meat pies, like mugs of hot soup, double as hand warmers and are delicious when you are outside. In fact, this is about the only time for a meat pie, I think. Donna Hay has a recipe called 'lunchbox pies' in her Food Fast book, but you could easily find something in your local shops. Subject bought pies to a little styling with foil and greaseproof tied with string and pop them in an enamel lunch tin to keep warm.

A camping stove is good for a winter picnic – not only is one mightily grateful for a flame, but gathering around it is also quite festive. Armed with one of these, the opportunities are endless and you can start getting quite elaborate with your lunches – an al fresco fry-up, for example. Storm kettles, designed for fishermen so that they could boil water in gales, are just what you need for the blustery picnic if you like a fresh brew. You do need some twigs and things for making a fire for this, so its appeal depends slightly on how hearty you intend getting.

If hunter-gathering is not really your thing, you can go equipped with one of those mini-fridges-cum-heaters that plug into the power socket of your car. Keeping drinks icy in summer and soup warm in winter is a luxury worth the investment, I think.

Finally, I don't think that there is anything more welcome anywhere, ever, than a Thermos of hot sausages. Always remember the mustard.

The jellied stock in the following recipe freaks me out a bit, as I just can't get my head around all that boiling, and when you are about to go on a picnic you don't really have time. I used a tin of chicken broth, and then made up some vegetable stock from bouillon powder and it was all delicious. I chucked in some beef consommé at the end too. Sorry Tamasin!! I know that one's soup is only as good as one's stock and a good chicken stock is quite easy to make, but really good jellied stocks are the territory of great cooks who make them and use them a lot. The soup comes up quite thin the way I made it, but I recommend you treat it like a good tomato juice and turn it into a hot bloody Mary – excellent when you are out in the cold. But remember not to add the vodka until you are ready to drink it. It will just evaporate otherwise.

EASY ROAST CHERRY TOMATO SOUP

(courtesy of Tamasin Day-Lewis)

1kg organic cherry tomatoes

3 fat cloves of garlic in their skins

1.2 litres intense jellied chicken stock; made by poaching 2 fowl and then making a further stock from the carcasses and poaching liquor with vegetables (but see my note on the previous page)

1 heaped teaspoon muscovado sugar

salt and pepper

- Roast the tomatoes in a roasting tin with the garlic for about an hour in a medium oven. The skins will have split, and the juices run.
- Allow the tomatoes to cool until you can handle them, then skin them and the garlic, and put in the blender with 2–3 ladles of the hot stock. Whizz then sieve, including the skins which you can press the flavour from.
- Return to the pan with the rest of the stock, add the sugar and the seasoning to taste, and serve. I resist the usual urge for basil, butter, cream or parsley. This is an intensely enough flavoured soup as it is, and utterly simple to make.

CHEESE AND THYME SCONES

(courtesy of Tamasin Day-Lewis)

Makes 12 scones

225g organic strong white flour
1 teaspoon baking powder
40g butter
a pinch of salt
125g coarsely grated good strong Cheddar
1 teaspoon of mustard powder
2 teaspoons of fresh thyme leaves
a pinch of cayenne pepper
150ml of milk

- Preheat oven to 200°C/gas mark 6
- Rub the butter into the sifted flour, salt and baking powder in a bowl. Bring your hands high above the bowl while you are doing this as you have to keep air in the mix to keep it light.
- Add two-thirds of the coarsely grated cheese and the mustard, thyme and cayenne, and then gradually cut the milk in with a knife; you might not need it all but you want a soft dough.
- Roll out to 1.5cm thickness, then cut out the scones with an upturned glass or pastry cutter
- Put the scones on a buttered baking tray, sprinkle with the remaining cheese, and bake for 12–15 minutes. Set on a wire rack for 5 minutes, then eat hot with lashings of country butter.

THE SWEET END

THE SWEET END

I'm always ready for something sweet at the end of dinner and find the idea of no pudding frankly devastating. There are very few people who don't love pudding, especially if someone else has done the work for them. It doesn't have to be a lot – a few macaroons, Florentines, or even delicious fruit are extremely welcome. I am afraid that I'm no longer a fan of the fruit tart, the one that has been purchased at the very smart bakery round the corner. Somehow it has become rather boring and my anticipation turns to slight disappointment when it appears. Even more disappointingly (for my bottom), I still eat it.

ICE CREAM

OK, so there is nothing very ground-breaking about ice cream. But there are things you can do to make it rather more exciting than usual. For starters, ice cream is much better served in delicious round scoops in a lovely big bowl, instead of having to be chiselled out of the tub at the table. There's nothing more ordinary than a plastic tub and pudding should be anything but ordinary. If the ice cream is soft enough, scoop it out with a tablespoon to get those wonderful lozenge shapes you get in restaurants. Another of my favourite things is to put a scoop of really good vanilla ice cream in a small glass tumbler and pour a cup of espresso over it. The coffee needs to be cold or cool or it melts the ice cream too quickly. Vanilla icebergs are rather good though. When the ice cream is so frozen you can hardly get it out of the tub and you have to attack it with a knife, you get iceberg shapes and these are delicious dumped in your cup of coffee – like a sophisticated Coke-float.

Special flavours

Keep a look out for good flavours of ice cream. If you can find something different to what is usually on offer, then you are on to something. Lebanese restaurants often have delicious ice creams and sorbets, flavoured with things like orange blossom or pistachio.

Ice creams and sorbets are usually wonderful colours, so have some fun when you are deciding what to serve. You could buy tubs of strawberry, vanilla and chocolate and scoop them into a bowl, like the stripy Neapolitan ice cream that you never see any more – do you remember that when you were at school?

A wonderful combination is green tea ice cream with chocolate sauce. The two flavours work very well together, and you could use bitter chocolate ice cream to serve with the green tea ice cream instead of chocolate sauce, if you like – or serve it as well. Try your local Thai restaurant for the ice cream and ask if you can get some to take away or if they know where to buy it; or see page 255 for stockists. The two colours look good together so think carefully about what colour bowl to use. Have a little dish of cookies on the table too – you need little extras to make ice cream a bit special.

ICE CREAM IS MUCH BETTER SERVED IN DELICIOUS ROUND SCOOPS IN A LOVELY BIG BOWL, INSTEAD OF HAVING TO BE CHISELLED OUT OF THE TUB AT THE TABLE.

Syrups and sauces

Check specialist shops for good syrups. There are lots of fudge and chocolate ones available, and I found a delicious vanilla-and-caramel-flavoured syrup recently. It's extremely good added to your coffee or poured over ice cream or sharp fruit (not fruit tart) – just poach or bake some plums for a few minutes, or cook them in a hot pan face down. Simple vanilla ice cream with good runny honey is really yummy, and golden syrup is the best. Vanilla ice cream with muscovado and cream is really good.

Another recent discovery of mine is a very good banana and brown sugar ice cream with a little Frangelico poured over the top. Frangelico is a hazelnut liqueur, which sounds grotesque but is actually rather delicious over ice cream. Now, I like to transfer the liqueur into a small decanter, partly because the style jury is still out on the bottle Frangelico comes in, which is the shape of a friar complete with rope belt. It is quite hysterical, but I think that people are more likely to try the liqueur if it's decanted. It certainly looks more appealing and more like a syrup, and some people might be prejudiced against flavoured liqueurs.

Frangelico is a hazelnut liqueur, which sounds grotesque but is actually rather delicious over ice cream.

FRUIT AND CREAM

I would be the first person to yawn at the idea of fruit and cream for pudding. I like plenty of e numbers in my sweets and sugar in my puddings. But you can spin some tricks with fruit and come up with yummy options and they aren't hard. My best friend Honor's mother used to make this delicious grape gratin pudding. Cut some seedless grapes in half and lay them in a gratin dish with Greek yoghurt poured over the top. Sprinkle on some brown sugar and put the dish under the grill – the crunchy brown sugar is the best bit of this. There's only one tricky bit: you need to peel the grapes, which is laborious, and if you have children I would bribe them to do this for you. Otherwise, that's the extent of the recipe, but it is utterly delicious and somehow tastes vaguely healthy. You can vary it according to the time of year and the fruit available. Grapes are pretty good all year, but you could use red fruit or peaches and nectarines.

Cream – and how to make it even naughtier and even nicer

You will find these cream ideas attached to puddings throughout this chapter, but they are good to have listed together so that you can find them easily. I don't think that they should necessarily be kept strictly with specific puddings they are shown with – you might even find the pudding surplus to requirements, depending on what you are up to.

Vanilla cream

This is delicious. If you can get hold of a vanilla pod, scrape the insides into a bowl of cream and beat it until it has thickened slightly. Always do this in a mixing bowl and then decant the cream into something pretty like a small glass bucket, an oversized rummer or a pretty creamware bowl. There's nothing nicer than seeing an undisturbed bowl of cream with a silver spoon sitting in it.

Soured cream and brown sugar

This is one of the best things ever. You just can't believe that it is so simple and, more to the point, soooooooooo delicious. Make a lot of it. Pour soured cream into a bowl and add soft brown muscovado sugar to taste. I feel obliged to serve this with fruit (see peaches and cream on page 238), but people are happy to spoon it straight from the bowl into their mouths.

Amaretto cream

My friend Phil suggests serving this with warm figs, but it is good with other things too. You could use something other than amaretto, like Frangelico. Break some amaretti biscuits over the top before serving.

Crème fraîche

This doesn't need anything doing to it: just scoop it out

of the tub and put it in a glass or bowl. It is delicious and especially good with very sweet puddings. I am not a fan of those doughy fruit tarts, as I said, but a galette is quite different. It is a tart with very thin pastry and finely sliced apples or plums covered with a glaze – delicious with crème fraîche.

Seasonal fruits

Anything that you have to wait for is usually good, so seasonal things make excellent treats. We can buy most things all year round, but there is nothing like the spring and summer for the most delicious fresh fruit – eating cherries or peaches in the winter is weird and they're not usually any good. When you shop, try to buy the best available produce and keep it simple. Good fruit in its season needs very little help to be appealing and during the strawberry and raspberry season there is little point in eating anything else.

Berries and crème fraîche mixed with caster sugar is one of my favourite puddings and takes some beating on the taste front. I like to put three bowls of fruit on the table, maybe raspberries, blackberries and blueberries, if you can catch them together, so people can help themselves. If you are going to serve berries, do make sure that you've tasted them in the shop and I highly recommend going to a greengrocer to buy them rather than a supermarket. You can find very good produce in supermarkets, but I'm not sure what happens when you start tasting the fruit, although you can usually tell a good strawberry by smelling it.

Fruit and rice pudding

There are so many good ready-made rice puddings on the market that you don't have to make your own. But I am a great believer in buying something and adding a bit of something to it. If you poach some fruit, like the plums I mentioned above, serve a plum in the top of each bowl of rice pudding. It will look delicious, taste pretty good and no one will think for a minute that you didn't make it all yourself. Make sure that you decant the pudding into one of your own dishes before putting it in the oven to heat up.

Peaches and cream

I first found this recipe in a *Donna Hay* magazine (an Australian food magazine that is so inspiring and hip; it makes Martha Stewart look like Betty Crocker). It takes no time at all and has always been a wild success, so I highly recommend you get the hang of it. Buy a peach for each guest, maybe a few extras. Before dinner, cut them in half and dip them face down into a plate of soft brown sugar. Leave them there until you are ready for pudding. Pour some soured cream into a bowl, the quantity depending on number of guests. (The other night I used two 284ml tubs for 12 people and there was enough.) Sweeten the soured cream with soft brown sugar and stir until it is all dissolved. Keep tasting it until it is sweet enough, but be careful not to over sweeten, as it is the balance between the slightly bitter cream and the sugar that is so good. Make a lot of this because it is delicious and the fruit is really just a vehicle for the cream.

When you are ready to serve pudding, put a dry frying pan on the heat. When it's hot, pop the peaches in face down and leave them until they are hot, soft and slightly caramelised. Give everyone two peach halves and a generous serving of cream – I serve this without really asking if anyone would like any. Peaches and cream sounds like a really dull pudding, but everyone will be thrilled when they taste this version. Plums or apricots also work well, but I would avoid using very sweet fruits like mangoes or pineapple, as they get a bit sickly.

Anything that you have to wait for is usually good, so seasonal things make excellent treats.

Black figs and amaretto cream

Figs are so good, but you must get them in season when they are sweet and juicy. This is a favourite of my friend Phil – the king of simple and delicious cooking. Warm some black figs in the oven until they are hot and soft, then slice them in two. Mix some crème fraîche or double cream with amaretto (that liqueur in the seventies-style bottle) and serve on top of the warm caramelised figs.

Because figs go so well with cheese this is the perfect thing to serve if you want to combine your cheese and pudding courses. They will look lovely on the table together and very often people want either cheese or pudding, not both.

BREAD AND BUTTER PUDDING

I was taught to make this by a man called Marcus, who worked in the house where I had my first job. I was the research assistant to Meredith (whose house it was) and Marcus was the butler/gardener/cook/valet/dog walker/nanny and just about everything else. When I got bored with what I was doing I would go downstairs and help him polish Meredith's husband's shoes, learning how to spit and polish. I also learned how to make this pudding and I still have the recipe in my old notebook.

There aren't that many occasions you can serve this heart-stopping pudding. It is far too much to have in the evening and most women reel in horror at the sight of it, as you can feel your bottom grow just looking at it. Sunday lunch is a good time and you can prepare it on Saturday. Marcus makes it in a soufflé dish so that it rises up like a soufflé instead of being flat, like B & B pudding usually is. I think this might be the reason that it is such an undertaking to eat. I hate normal custard, but this is something quite different. It is really more like crème anglaise, which is just French for custard, but thinner and better than those jugs of yellow wobble that I spent my childhood avoiding. Your eyes will roll to the back of your head with pleasure as you feel this custard trying to course through your arteries. I know that this is not supposed to be any girl's aim, but if you are in a position where you want to seduce an Englishman with a sweet tooth, try this custard. One mouthful and he will be on his knees! It is questionable whether you want your skills in the kitchen to be what clinches the deal, but it's good to have up your sleeve.

To make the custard (this is enough for 8–10 people but you can always halve it):

1 litre double cream
8 eggs
450g caster sugar
1 vanilla pod

- Bring the cream to the boil with the vanilla pod.
- Put the eggs and sugar in a bowl and beat together.
- Pour the hot cream into the egg and sugar through a sieve. Put the bowl of custard over a pan of simmering water, don't let the bowl touch the water, and heat over a low flame until it is thick. It should take about half an hour, so be patient.

I have, of course, tried to make this more quickly and ended up with very sweet and creamy scrambled eggs! You don't want it to cook; you are just heating it. You cannot leave this custard; you have to stand over it, which is why people think it is hard. Frankly, though, standing over it is easier. What I find impossible is remembering to go back to something. I go off and start something else, forgetting all about the cooking until I can smell it burning. There's no chance of forgetting something you are standing over, so try this, but keep the rest of the meal simple so you don't give yourself too much work.

Back to the pudding

Originally this pudding was designed to use up stale bread, but I can never do that because I never have any food in the house unless people are coming to dinner. The best thing is to get the bread in advance so that it is a day old when you come to use it. You need quite a light bread for this; a normal white sliced loaf is not going to work because it is too dense. The best is day-old French bread, which you can get cheap when it is stale – how marvellous that this pudding is actually economical. Marcus recommends panettone, which everyone has lying around after Christmas. Don't use brown bread, he says, or anything that is too doughy.

Leave the butter out of the fridge so that it is soft for easy spreading. Slice some bread, butter it on both sides and start lining the soufflé dish with it. Put some raisins or sultanas in between the slices intermittently, depending on how much you like them. Marcus suggests using dried apricots, but only if you prepare the mixture and leave it to soak the night before, otherwise they are like bullets. As you layer the bread in the dish, pour in some custard so it can start soaking into the bread, but don't pour in so much that the bread is floating. I sometimes spread some marmalade on the bread, and I often suggest that cinnamon might be nice, but these ideas always get the same response from Marcus. In his very deep and very proper voice, he says, 'don't go whoring after new taste sensations'. Of course I am always trying to do precisely that, but I think he has a point. Have you ever had chocolate bread and butter pudding in fancy restaurants It never tastes as good as the original one.

Once the bread comes to the top of your dish and you've poured in all the custard, add a few last slices of bread and scatter some brown sugar on the top. Cover the dish with a damp tea towel so the bread doesn't dry out and leave – overnight if you like.

When you're ready to cook the pudding, put it in a hot oven for about an hour or until done – whichever comes first. Test it with a metal skewer: if it comes out dry, the pudding is done. I like it to be a little gooey, so if you like that too, bring it out a little early. Serve with a jug of extra custard. I know this is a big-deal recipe but it is worth it. People rarely have these old-fashioned puddings so something like this really blows them away.

BYPASSING PUDDING

The easiest way to do pudding is to go shopping for some good treats for serving with good herbal tea or coffee. I am constantly on the look-out for treats, but that is because I am hopelessly greedy and have a sweeter tooth than a small child. The great thing about this sort of shopping is that it requires NO culinary expertise, no faffing about and sweet things don't usually go off very quickly. This opens up the possibilities because you can bring little things back from your travels. When I go to some amazing deli with people who are good cooks, they go crazy about the wonderful polenta or white beans or any of those store-cupboard things, but I just freeze in fear. I have no idea how to turn any of it into anything. But show me a dish piled high with macaroons and I can tell you right away if they are any good. Then all I have to do is decide is how many I want and think about what sort of plate to put them on and who to offer them to. That is my sort of cooking – buying and serving. It sounds silly I know, but once you start thinking this way you will find very interesting things, and you will be able to knock the socks off the fancy show-offs with their beans and polenta – sweet treats are so much prettier.

Start looking close to home

Always keep your eyes open for new things. Recently I have found the most devilish Florentines at my local baker; they are extremely chewy and totally delicious. I also found some marshmallows at the most stylish farm shop in the middle of Gloucestershire. They are not your usual marshmallows but very special, melt-in-your-mouth ones, made by a master patissier. The thing with treats is that they can be quite ordinary on the face of it, but they have got to have something about them that is unusual or special. It doesn't always have to be fanciness – it can be as simple as novelty value.

Marshmallows, for example – serve them as they are in a pretty bowl or add them to a cup of rich hot chocolate. To make the sort of hot chocolate you are going to want at the end of dinner, melt some chocolate with a very high cocoa content (70 per cent) in a bowl over some simmering water. Add a little hot, frothed-up milk – you just want to thin the chocolate so that it is easier to drink, making velvety liquid chocolate rather than a big milky drink. Just before serving, drop a marshmallow into the cup. Offer this drink in small cups: it's very delicious but very rich. See also pages 165–6.

Going along the treats route means you can put several bowls of things on the table for everyone to pick at. While many people are too full for a proper pudding in the evening, they love a few tiny treats, which make a delightful conclusion to a meal. I think that picking encourages chat and you don't have to concentrate like you do if you're eating pudding. I love sitting at the end of dinner chatting, with my hand almost permanently in a bowl of chocolate-coated orange rind, almond tuiles or yoghurt-covered raisins.

The important thing here is the size. Treats need to be bite-sized so people aren't afraid to take them. Many people, especially girls, are embarrassed to have too much of a fattening thing on their plate. For example, Florentines are often rather large and far too much for someone to eat at the end of dinner, but you can find boxes of mini-florentines in some delis and even supermarkets. If you can only find big ones, just break them up. You can do the same with giant cookies.

TREATS NEED TO BE BITE-SIZED SO PEOPLE AREN'T AFRAID TO TAKE THEM.

Finding fabulousness in aisle 12

The great thing about chocolate as an end-of-dinner treat is that you can serve everything from the very best to the cheap stuff you find in the newsagents; it all has its moment. I found mini ice-cream chocolates the other day while I was spinning a trolley around the supermarket and they made the perfect treat with coffee. I really enjoy checking the chocolate aisle in the supermarket for things that can be made stylish and often I think people love to be offered the old favourites – the chocolate bars they used to love as children.

The broken bar

A broken-up chocolate bar is one of my favourite things to put on a coffee tray or in the middle of the table. It is so easy and looks really stylish. Look for organic chocolate bars, which now come in all sorts of interesting flavours. For something even more special you have to plan ahead and go to special chocolate shops – many offer online ordering.

Fancy chocs

If you are ever in Paris, make sure that you don't leave without going to Fouquet, a place that gets my heart beating and adrenalin pumping (see page 255 for details). A specialist chocolate shop, it is a by-word in understated style and their packaging is wonderful. People in the know will faint with delight when you produce a jar of their pastel-coloured mini-mints, pecans in caramel, bergamot boiled sweets or melt-on-the-tongue truffles. One of my favourite things is chocolate-coated orange rind chocolate, which is easy to find, but at Fouquet they do grapefruit rind. This is what Fouquet is like – always just a little bit more chic.

The best things they do – I think – are their tins of sweets, which are made at the back of the shop; the tins come in three different sizes and wonderful colours like apple green, candy pink, baby blue, fire-engine red, Hermès orange, bitter-chocolate brown. Fouquet also

sell chocolate powder for making hot chocolate, and there is a wide range to choose from, depending on when and how it is to be drunk. They have powder, flakes or granules, different cocoa contents and on and on. It is really the loveliest shop.

I can't do round-the-world chocolate shops, but if you should visit Vienna, do go to Demel. It is a marvellously old-fashioned chocolate shop and the chocolates come in the most wonderful boxes, which are painted with violets. Demel used to provide the

GOOEY MACAROONS ARE ANOTHER EYE-ROLLING-TO-THE-BACK-OF-YOUR-HEAD EXPERIENCE, MY BENCHMARK OF A GOOD THING.

Austrian Empress with crystallised violets, so these are one of their specialities, but their regular boxes of chocolates are made from the same recipes and to the same standards as they were in the 18th century.

You never know where you're going to find good chocolates. I found a brilliant sweet shop the other day in Kingussie in Scotland. They had big jars of proper old-fashioned sweets like sour plums and acid drops. If these tickle your fancy, look at this website: aquarterof.com. They have virtually every sweet that ever existed, and you are bound to find something that you could have with coffee. I have just placed an order for violet buds, chocolate satins, things called Granny sookers which look like jewels – they are purple and green and look wonderful in a little glass jar on the table.

And fancy macaroons

While you are in Paris, you should also stop by Ladurée (see page 255 for details) for a box of their macaroons. If you are planning to have people for dinner when you get home, buy two boxes. It isn't possible to sit on the train with a box of these without trying one. And once you have tried one you will have to eat all of them, because you just can't help it. They come in loads of flavours and the colours are amazing – greens, pinks, purples, bright yellow, coffee and neutral colours.

You can also find good macaroons in delis and bakers in places other than Paris. Ottolenghi in London do delicious flavours – traditionally, raspberry, chocolate, coffee, pistachio or vanilla, but also more exotic ones now like orange blossom, lime and basil, cappuccino, banana and chocolate. If possible, try macaroons in the shop; they are only good when they are gooey. If they are overcooked or even a day old they will be crunchy like meringues, which is really no good at all. Gooey macaroons are another eye-rolling-to-the-back-of-your-head experience, my benchmark of a good thing.

All these after-dinner treats are good things to take to someone else's house when you're going for dinner. They are easy to add to the table and they are delicious, which makes them the perfect thing. I find that as I get older there are some places where I take a bottle of wine and others where wine isn't right but I still want to take something – and this is where the macaroons come in very handy.

COFFEE

I am getting keener and keener on serving coffee and pudding at the same time. In the evening, people don't always want a big pudding and it is lovely to have a light pudding on little glass plates with coffee. Serve some frothy hot milk so people can have espressos or macchiatos. Also make a pot of herbal tea. If no one wants either simply serve your pudding and perhaps offer coffee with chocolates a bit later.

Many more people have espresso machines now and these make fancy coffee easy. I am not a huge fan of the coffee plunger and I really hate filter coffee. In addition to my espresso pot, I am very attached to my latte whisk or milk plunger; I have both so that if one is out of action I have a back-up. Serve coffee in glasses,

mugs or cups. Once you get into the styling, you will take as much pleasure in what you drink from as you will from the coffee itself.

Espresso

This is obviously the easiest one to serve. Instead of having to faff about with the milk frother it is a one-hit wonder. Keep an eye out for lovely espresso cups. I have just bought some that are like mini beakers – white on the outside and different colours on the inside, and they come with a little ceramic spoon and saucer.

Macchiatos and noisettes

A noisette is a French name for a small coffee with a little milk; a macchiato in Italy. Make a pot of coffee and heat and froth a jugful of milk and you can offer all these choices. I turn into a café owner, standing in front of the coffee machine, making up all these different varieties. Serve in small glasses or espresso cups.

Lattes

Now I don't want to sound bossy – God forbid – but people shouldn't be drinking these at night; it is just too much milk. I used to serve lattes in tumblers, because it was something different to cups and saucers and I liked the layers you get with the coffee and the froth, but I have changed my view. I think lattes should be served in teacups, like a not-so-frothy cappuccino. The same goes for the cappuccino crowd – they get a teacup and saucer too, like a frothier latte. They look much prettier served like this than they do in glasses. But it's to do with current style. When you tire of one way, change to the next.

Whatever you do, do it with conviction. I was talking to a friend of mine recently about how much we like instant coffee. It is an excellent drink, but the mistake people make is to compare it with proper coffee. I often find myself asking for an instant coffee at the end of dinner. People look a bit stunned at first and then do one of two things: they go and look for some –a lot of people don't have any in the house any more – or they heave a sigh of relief and produce the jar. A mug of instant with milk and sugar or caff style with hot milk is lovely.

TEA

If you serve tea, always make it in a pot. There is nothing worse than listening to that long list of flavoured teas, which all sound like puddings or Thai soup, and then seeing a cup of hot water coming across the table with a loose bag. Even worse is dealing with the soggy tea bag that always sends up in the ashtray. I avoid offering too many flavours; make the choice of tisane flavour yourself. If you aren't as naturally bossy as me, ask whether fennel or whatever is OK. I don't think any of those teas taste of much, but fennel is good, and it goes straight through you, which, after a heavy dinner, is much appreciated. Verveine or jasmine are also good teas to have at night. Avoid camomile: it smells of old flower water and tastes of it, too.

INDEX

autumn parties 176–7

bed
breakfast in 58–9, 69
tea or coffee in 59
birthday breakfasts 68
birthday dinners 117, 161
bowls
for coffee 53–4
for dips 133
salad bowls 30–1, 98–9
as serving dishes 100
breakfasts 50–73
in bed 58–9, 69
birthdays 68
for children 166–7
Christmas 68–9
cooked 60–7
Easter 70–2
everyday 52–5
St Valentine's Day 179–80
Saturday morning for two 55–7
buffets 87–8, 185–200
cold buffet tables 185–96
hot dishes 197–200
simpler tables 196

camping stoves 226–7
candlelight 96
carafes 81–2
celebrations 174–200
autumn parties 176–7
buffets 185–200
Mother's Day 183–4
personal 177–8
St Valentine's Day 178–82
spring parties 176, 177
children 162–73
breakfasts 166–7
Easter 70–1
drinks 164, 165–6
lunches 167–9
puddings 170
teatime 171–2
china platters 80–1
Christmas breakfasts 68–9
cocktail napkins 135
cups
coffee cups 78
French breakfast cups 53
cushions, for picnics 222–3
cutlery
buying 77
for picnics 212

dahlias 93
Day-Lewis, Tamasin, recipes from 228–9
dinner parties 110–61
aperitifs 123–8
birthday dinners 117, 161
canapés and pre-dinner treats 129–34
chaos in the kitchen 159
cheese course 156–8
cocktail napkins 135
disasters 159
dress 119
extra guests 118
fitting people round the table 114
getting organised 122–3
inviting people 112–13, 114–18
latecomers 17, 160
main courses 136–55
pacing yourself 159
shopping for 120–1
thank you letters 160–1
see also guests
dishes, heart-shaped 181

Easter breakfast 70–3
eggcups 60
enamel mugs for picnics 212–13
espresso machines 53
etiquette 20

farmer's markets 32, 120
fireside tea trays 104–5
flowers
on outdoor tables 204
table decorations 93–5
thanking someone with 161
food shopping 83–8

gardenias 94–5
girlfriends, lunch at home with 31–7
glasses 54, 81, 82, 98
guests
arriving 17, 18
breakfast in bed for 58–9
cancelling 15, 21
deciding on 12–13
entertaining in-laws and other VIPs 43–6
etiquette 20
first timers 21
formality or informality with 23–4
friend thieving 21
how to be an easy guest 18–19
introductions 22–3
invitations 14–16
leaving 17, 19

Hay, Donna 132, 226
home shopping 77–82

in-laws 43–6, 59
introductions 22–3
invitations 14–16

late-night trays 105–7
lighting 96–7
for eating outdoors at night 205
lunches
for children 167–9
with a girlfriend at home 31–7
Mother's Day 183–4
outdoors 204–5

markets 76, 77
melamine platters 80
Mother's Day 183–4
mothers-in-law 46
mugs for picnics 212–13

napkins
breakfast 58, 65, 67
buying 78–9
cocktail 135
St Valentine's Day 180–1
tea towels as 65, 106
night, eating outdoors at 205

outdoor eating 202–29
at night 205
drinks 206, 210
lunches 204–5, 208
summer 208
winter 208–10
see also picnics

picnics 210–29
cutlery and plates 212–13
food 214–19
packing for 210–11, 213–14
shopping for equipment 211
summer 220–5
winter 225–9
pint glasses 54, 82
plates
buying 77–8
for picnics 212
platters 31, 80–1, 99, 100
presents
birthday 117, 160
Easter 71–2
puddings 232–43
bypassing pudding 243–9
for children 170
Sunday lunches 183–4

RSVP 15–16

St Valentine's Day 178–82
salad bowls and platters 30–1, 98–9
serving dishes 97–8
shopping 8, 76–88
arriving home with 88
for chocolate 246–7
for dinner parties 120–1
food 83–8
home 77–82
spring parties 176, 177
Stevens, Gail, buffet recipes from 189–94
summer lunches 208
summer picnics 220–5
Sunday evening suppers 38–42
Sunday lunches, Mother's Day 183–4
supermarket shopping 121
suppers
Sunday evening 38–42
weekday 25–30
sweet peas 93–4

table settings 90–101
breakfasts 58, 65, 67, 72–3
candlelight 96
colour schemes 92, 100–1
flowers 93–5, 204
lighting the room 96–7
serving dishes 97–8
serving styles 99–101
see also napkins; trays
tablecloths
buying 78–9
Easter breakfasts 72–3
outdoor eating 204
tables for outdoor eating 204–5, 206

tea cosies 101
tea sets 101
tea towels 65, 106–7
teapots 104–5
teatime for children 171–2
thank you letters 160–1
toast racks 55, 104–5, 180, 181
tray cloths 107
trays
breakfast in bed 58
eating off 101–7
late-night 105–7
tea trays 104–5

weekday suppers 25–30
weekend guests 48
winter
eating outdoors in 208–10
picnics 225–9

INDEX OF RECIPES AND FOOD IDEAS

almond milk 206
amaretto cream 236
with black figs 239
Americano 125
apples 120, 158
artichoke hearts 134
asparagus 137
aubergine dip (moutabal) 32, 131
avocados 223, 224–5

bacon
breakfast 59, 60
butties 63
egg and bacon baps 63
baked eggs 42
beans
white bean dip 132–3
wild rice salad 189–92
beef
cold roast 196, 208
fillet of 137–8
never-fail chilli 208, 209
beet and horseradish sauce 196
Bellinis 124, 206
blinis 182
bloody bull 125
hot bloody bull shots 226
boiled eggs 60–1
at Easter 73
hard-boiled 34–6
bread
for breakfast 55
crostini 133–4
bread and butter pudding 184, 240–3
bread sauce 143–4
Brie 195
brioche 66
broccoli 154, 168
Brussels sprouts 183
butter, fancy 194
butterflied lamb 138–40
butternut squash, hot roasted 194

cakes
carrot cake 184, 216–19
cupcakes 172–3
fairy cakes 172, 173
picnic 215–19
Campari 126–7
carrot cake 184, 216–19
caviar 181–2
champagne 123–4
pink 206
Cheddar cheese 157, 195
cheese
autumn party 177
for buffets 195
buying 83, 121
Cheddar 157
cheese courses 45, 120, 156–8, 159
cheese and thyme scones 229
fruit with 158
in mashed potatoes 150
mozzarella salad 85, 145
Parmesan 134
plough girl's lunch 33
and pudding 239
salads with 156, 157, 158
sandwiches 105–6
Stilton 157
vacherin 157
chicken
bread sauce with 143–4
carving 142
for children 168, 169
coronation 189
pies 86
roast 43, 142–5, 168, 183, 188
at buffets 188
for children 168
summer 144–5
winter 142–4
chips, fish and 168–9
chocolate 164
after-dinner treats 245–8
broken-up bars 246
green tea ice cream with chocolate sauce 233
hot 165–6, 244–5
chutney 33, 157, 196
cocktails 124–6
coffee
after-dinner 249–50
breakfast 53–5
espresso 53, 54, 250
with ice cream 232–3
instant 251
lattes 53, 54, 251
sweet treats to serve with 243–9
courgettes 154–5
crab 32, 83, 220, 221
cracked eggs 42
cream
amaretto cream 236, 239
and fruit 84, 98, 235–9
soured cream and brown sugar 236
vanilla cream 236
crème fraîche 237
crostini 133–4
crudités 130–2
cupcakes 172–3
curries 38, 40, 87
Thai green 45–6

dates 195
deli food 32, 84, 131, 133
dressed crab 32, 83, 220, 221
drinks 123–8
almond milk 206
Campari 126–7
champagne 123–4, 206
for children
fizzy 164–5
milky 165–6
cocktails 124–6
gin and vodka tonics 128
hot drinks for outdoors 210
non-alcoholic 128, 206
shandy 206
summer 206

Easter eggs 71–2
eggs
baked 42
boiled 60–1, 73, 167
hard-boiled 34–6
cracked 42
Easter 71–2
egg and bacon baps 63
fried
full English breakfast 64
heart-shaped 179–80
giant breakfast 62
with ham 65
mini breakfasts 167
omelettes 41–2
pickled 214–15
quails' 167
Scotch eggs 83, 213–14
scrambled 59, 66–7, 106
endive salad 148
English breakfast 63–4, 65
espresso coffee 53, 54, 250

fairy cakes 172, 173
figs 85
black figs with amaretto cream 239
fish 150–3
buying 153
and chips 168–9
salmon 150–2, 153
sea bass 152–3
trout 153
tuna 34
Florentines 232, 244, 245
Frangelico 234–5
French bean salad 26–7
French toast 66
fruit
with cheese 120, 158
compotes 57, 180
and cream 84, 98, 235–9
galettes 237
nectars 124, 128, 206
seasonal 237
tarts 232

garlic, roast 143
gin and tonic 128
grapes
with Greek yoghurt 235
Muscat 158, 195
green bean salad 148
green salad 145

ham
breakfast 64–5
whole cooked 188
hard-boiled eggs 34–6
herbal tea 243, 249, 252
herbs in salads 145, 183, 223–4
hot chocolate 165–6, 244–5

ice cream 232–5
sandwiches 170
syrups and sauces for 234–5

jam 55–6, 57
making 105
sandwiches 171

lamb
butterflied 138–40
lamb chops and salad 141–2
rack of 43–4
roast 183
shepherd's pie 86, 167–8, 197–200
lasagne, ready-made 86, 107
leeks, sautéed 155
lettuce 36, 222
lobsters 182, 221

macaroons 232, 248–9
marshmallows 244?5
membrillo (quince jelly) 158
milk
breakfast 56
milky drinks for children 165–6
moutabal (aubergine dip) 32, 131
mozzarella salad 85, 145
Muscat grapes and raisins 158, 195
mushrooms
baked eggs 42
on toast 38, 64

oatcakes 45, 121, 157, 195
plough girl's lunch 33
okra, sautéed 155
omelette and salad 41–2
orange breakfast platter 62
orange juice 54

pancakes 66
pasta 27–9
for children 169
serving 29
spaghetti with garlic, chilli and bacon 176–7
tomato sauce for 27, 28
peaches and cream 238–9
pears 120, 158
peas 130, 183
peppers, pimientos de Padrón 132
pickled eggs 214–15
pickled walnuts 195
picnic food 214–21
cakes 215–19
summer picnics 220–1, 223–5
winter picnics 225–9
pies 83, 86
meat 226
pork 83, 213–14
pink champagne 206
plough girl's lunch 33
plums 237, 238
pork pies 83, 213–14
porridge 61–2
potatoes
baked 26–7, 182, 194
mashed 148–50
potato salads 193
roast new 137, 140, 143, 183
potted shrimps 32, 39, 83, 85, 220
prosciutto 65

quails' eggs 167
quince kelly (*membrillo*) 158

rack of lamb 43–4
radishes 130
raisins, muscat 158
raspberries
and cream 84, 237
raspberry jam 105
ready-made meals 40–1
cannelloni 86
lasagne 86, 197
see also take-away food
rice
and ready-made meals 40
rice pudding and fruit 238
risotto 37
salads 189, 192
wild rice salad 189–92
rocket salad 44–5, 85, 138
rotisserie chickens 86

salads
autumn party 177
for buffets 189–93
with cheese 156, 157, 158
dressings 29–30, 37
endive 148
French bean 26–7
from delis 32, 84
green 145
green bean salad 148
lamb chops and salad 141–2
mozzarella 85, 145
omelette and salad 41–2
outdoor eating 208
potato salads 193
rice 189, 192
rocket salad 44–5, 85, 137
salade niçoise 34–7
summer picnics 223–5
to serve with chicken 145–8
tossing 30–1, 99
wild rice 189–92
salmon 150–2
sandwiches
cheese 105–6
hundreds and thousands 170
jam 171
picnic baps 214
tiny 171, 172
sausage rolls 83
sausages
bangers and mash 148–9
breakfast 64, 69
teatime 172
scones, cheese and thyme 229
Scotch eggs 83, 213–14
scrambled eggs 59, 66–7, 106
sea bass 152–3
shandy 206
shepherd's pie 86, 197–200
mini 167–8
shrimps, potted 32, 39, 83, 85, 220
side car 126
smoked salmon, and scrambled eggs 66
soda bread 104
soup 226, 227
easy roast cherry tomato soup 228
soured cream and brown sugar 236
spaghetti with garlic, chilli and bacon 176–7
spring onions 225
squash and chickpea stew 210
steak and kidney pies 86
stews 27
never-fail chilli 208, 209
Stilton cheese 157, 195
strawberries and cream 84, 98, 237
summer chicken 144–5
sushi 129, 134
sweets 248

take-away food
buffet 87–8
curries 38, 45–6, 87
Japanese 178
tapas 132
tea
after-dinner 251–2
green tea ice cream with chocolate sauce 233
herbal 243, 249, 251
making 101–4
Thai green curry 45–6
thyme, cheese and thyme scones 229
tomato sauce
cracked eggs in 42
for pasta 27, 28
tomato soup 226
easy roast cherry tomato soup 228
tomatoes
breakfast 64
chopped 133–4
mozzarella, tomato and basil salad 145
peeling 36
for picnics 223, 224
roasted cherry tomatoes 140–1
sun-blushed 134

vacherin 157
vanilla cream 236
vegetables
broccoli 154, 168
Brussels sprouts 183
buying 120
for children 168
courgettes 154–5
main course 136, 137, 154–5
mashed 149
peas 130, 183
pre-dinner treats 130–2, 134
with rack of lamb 44
roasted vegetables with chicken 143
sautéeing 155
in shepherd's pie 200
vegetarians 129, 136, 150
vine leaves, stuffed 176
vodka tonics 128

white bean dip 132–3
wild rice 210
salad 189–92
wild salmon 150–2
winter chicken 142–4

yoghurt
breakfast 56–7
grapes with Greek yoghurt 235

SHOPPING

Alfie's Antique Market and Church Street,
13–25 Church Street, London NW8 8DT
Tel: 020 7723 6066

Baker and Spice, 47 Denyer Street,
London SW3 8DA
Tel: 020 7589 4734

Blandford Fruiterers, 25 Blandford Street,
London W1
Tel: 020 7935 4262

Borough Market, 8 Southwark Street,
London SE1 1TL
Tel: 020 7407 1002
www.boroughmarket.org.uk

Covent Garden Flower Market, New Covent
Garden Market, London SW8 5NX
Tel: 020 7720 2211 Fax: 020 7622 5307

Daylesford Organic, Daylesford, Nr. Kingham,
Gloucestershire, GL56 0YG
Tel: 01608 731 700

Fouquet, 22 rue François 1er 75008
PARIS – FRANCE
Tel: 33 (0) 1 47 23 30 36
Fax: 33 (0) 1 47 23 30 56

The Ginger Pig, Borough Market 8,
Southwark Street, London SE1 1TL
Tel: 020 7403 4721

Hummingbird Café, 133 Portobello Road,
London W11 2DY
Tel: 020 7229 6446

Konditor & Cook, 22 Cornwall Road,
London SE1 8TW
Tel: 020 7261 0456
Fax: 020 7261 9021

La Fromagerie, 2-4 Moxon Street,
London W1U 4EW
Tel/Fax: 0207 935 0341

La Picena, 5 Walton Street, London SW3
Tel: 0207 584 6573

Labour and Wait, 18 Cheshire Street,
London E2 6EH
Tel: 020 7729 6253

Ladurée, 75 avenue des Champs Elysee,
75008 Paris
www.laduree.fr

L'Artisan du Chocolat, 89 Lower Sloane Street,
London SW1 8DA
Tel: 020 7824 8365

Marylebone Farmers Market,
Cramer Street Car Park, Off Marylebone
High Street, London W1
Open Sundays, 10am–2pm

Mr. Mustard, S.G.Mustard, Station Road,
Nethy Bridge, Inverness-shire, PH25 3DN
Tel: 01479 831245

Nicole Farhi Home, 17 Clifford Street,
London W1
Tel: 020 7499 8368

Ottolenghi, 63 Ledbury Road, London W11 2AD
Tel: 020 7727 1121

Rococo, 321 Kings Road, London SW3 5EP
Tel: 020 7352 5857

Summerill & Bishop, 100 Portland Road,
London W11 4LQ
Tel: 020 7221 4566

Tavola, 155 Westbourne Grove,
London W11 2RS
Tel: 020 7229 0571

Valvona & Crolla, 19 Elm Row,
Edinburgh EH7 4AA, Scotland.
Tel. 0131 556 6066
Fax 0131 556 1668

Wagashi Japanese Bakery, Unit 1c,
Connaught Business Centre, Malham Road,
London SE23 1AH
Tel: 0208 699 1393

Waitrose, 0800 188 884; www.ocado.com

ACKNOWLEDGEMENTS

I owe many thanks to many people for this book. Firstly I must thank Lizzy Kremer who at the time of selling this book was my very spoiling agent; she read, edited, mulled over and inspired when this was just an idea, then a proposal and finally here it is. Thank you very much.

Thank you Carey Smith for your enthusiasm and keenness to work on more titles with me; I am very lucky to have such a supportive publisher. Helen Hutton for being so adorable, helpful and calm, especially in the moments when I was far from any of those things.

Special thanks to Caz Hildebrand for making this book look so lovely. Thank you to Joy Gosney for doing such wonderful illustrations inside the book and to Sam Wilson for the cover.

Trying to write a book about food when you really don't know how to cook takes a lot of leaning on your friends and I have many to thank. Jane Leaver for her cooking lessons, Ellie Klein for her tips and editing and general loveliness, my mum for sharing her shepherd's pie recipe and my dad, the ultimate frustrated bartender, for his cocktail recipes. Marcus Wignall-Parry for his bread and butter pudding, John Burn for sharing his perfect pot of tea and Diane Drain for the cake lessons. Also to Phil Poynter who really taught me about the simplicity of a good piece of meat and salad, and thank you so much for reading the draft of this book like you did with *Domestic Bliss*. I am so grateful to Gail Stevens who owns the delicious Baker and Spice. She was extremely generous with her recipes and ideas – thank you very much.

Lastly and most of all I want to thank my very great friends Eck and Lucy Ogilvie-Grant, who so generously lent me their glorious wooden house, Glencarnie, where I wrote most of this book. Not only was it pure heaven being in Scotland for such long periods of time but it was fabulous to have Lucy so close by for consultations, which I am sure were more fun than research is supposed to be. Thank you, thank you, and it is to both of you that I would like to dedicate this book with very much love. x